S0-BRZ-531

# Preaching Values in Today's English Version

based on texts selected from

Good News for Modern Man

The New Testament in Today's English Version

David A.
MacLennan

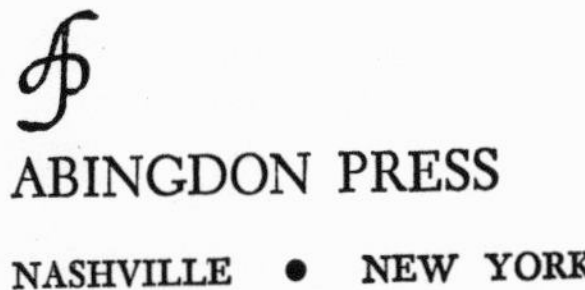

ABINGDON PRESS

NASHVILLE • NEW YORK

PREACHING VALUES IN TODAY'S ENGLISH VERSION



*ISBN* 0-687-33880-8

*Library of Congress Catalog Card Number:* 74-172811

## Acknowledgments

Grateful acknowledgment is made to the publishers of Bible text material cited by the author in the expositions of this book.

AMERICAN BIBLE SOCIETY
The Bible texts appearing in this publication, except when otherwise designated following the quotation, are from *Today's English Version of the New Testament*. Copyright © American Bible Society 1966. Used by permission.

THE MACMILLAN COMPANY
Scripture passages designated J. B. P. are from *The New Testament in Modern English,* translated by J. B. Phillips, copyright © J. B. Phillips 1958.

NATIONAL COUNCIL OF THE CHURCHES OF CHRIST IN THE U.S.A.
Scripture passages designated R.S.V. are from the *Revised Standard Version of the Bible,* copyright 1946 and 1952 by the Division of Christian Education of the National Council of Churches of Christ in the U.S.A., and are used by permission.

OXFORD AND CAMBRIDGE UNIVERSITY PRESSES
Scripture passages designated N.E.B. are from *The New English Bible,* © The Delegates of The Oxford University Press and The Syndics of The Cambridge University Press 1961, 1970.

SET UP, PRINTED, AND BOUND BY THE PARTHENON PRESS, AT NASHVILLE, TENNESSEE, UNITED STATES OF AMERICA

# Contents

# Introduction

"Phenomenal!" and "unprecedented!" are words of accurate response to the publishing figures concerning the most recent translation of the New Testament, *Good News for Modern Man—Today's English Version.* Translated from the Greek by Dr. Robert G. Bratcher, a research consultant in the translations department of the American Bible Society, this version was first scrutinized by a committee of twenty distinguished scholars. This committee suggested a number of revisions, but the published book is substantially the work of Dr. Bratcher. The TEV, as it is known by many readers, was first published by the American Bible Society in September, 1966. Bound in paper and priced at twenty-five cents, it was intended primarily for readers whose second language is English. It was also aimed at English-speaking persons to whom a scholarly translation would never appeal.

First printing was 150,000 copies; a cautious order. Subsequent demand and sales proved that it was one of the great underestimates of recent publishing. Made more appealing by line drawings by a gifted Swiss artist living in Paris, Mademoiselle Annie Vallotton, sales doubled, redoubled, tripled, and, as Dr. Webb Garrison said, "increased in geometric progression." Before its first year had ended, more than five million copies were in the hands of readers or being rushed to them. That it presented to readers of many countries and backgrounds "the true and lively Word" is demonstrated not only by the immense number of books sold but by the affectionate, sometimes colloquial, descriptions made by the not always silent majority. In the British Isles, because many copies were sold in food shops, it has been called "The Gospel of the Groceries." In Australia, some dubbed it "The Plain Jane Bible." In Canada and the United States, young people have praised it by calling it "The Swingers' Bible."

Results, some of them linked with therapy, have been most impressive. Patients and physicians have found TEV to convey what an ancient servant of Christ termed the sacrament of the Lord's Supper, "singular medicine for sick souls." Few paperback best sellers topped the TEV, and none of them have had the continued large sale of this clear, everyday speech translation of the New Testament. According to James Z. Nettinga, directing the American Bible Society's national distribution, in a relatively short time "that Testament in street clothes will hold the record as the best-selling paperbook ever issued." Facts support this claim. Before the third anniversary of its publication, TEV had come close to seventeen million copies sold.

It is an ecumenical edition: July 1969 saw a Roman Catholic edition with imprimatur of Cardinal Richard Cushing of Massachusetts. Southern Baptists ordered a special edition of one and a quarter million copies.

Deeply significant is the growing number of persons who testify that the living Word, even the divine Savior, drew near to them as they read and pondered this version of the Scriptures. God has used this translation to change lives. Surely the number of copies purchased and being read testifies to the hunger for the Word which in these revolutionary times few dreamed existed.

Over thirty years have passed since the late Professor Halford E. Luccock wrote and produced *Preaching Values in New Translations of the New Testament*. This book and its sequel, *Preaching Values in the Old Testament* (both published by Abingdon Press), meant much to preachers and teachers. Dr. Luccock's genius for the uncommon insight and illustration found many appreciative readers. When an editor invited me to do something similar to the outstanding books of my friend and former colleague at Yale, I accepted. Also, I realized that we must borrow Hal Luccock's title, or part of it, to accurately describe the purpose and content of this book.

Many of the suggestions first appeared in "Pulpit Patterns," a department of the recently deceased magazine for preachers, *The Pulpit*, published by the editors of *The Christian Century*. These "patterns" have been adapted and, I fondly hope, improved for this book. Others have been written for this volume.

The text used throughout this book is that of *Good News for Modern Man—Today's English Version*. Grateful acknowledgment is made to the American Bible Society and to Dr. Bratcher, who translated the basic text. Also I give my thanks to publishers and authors or authors' representatives who have permitted the use of quotations from their works. If any have been overlooked, I express sincere regret and will make amends in the next edition.

My thanks are given to several persons, but chiefly to Guy Brown. Without his encouragement, patience, and research, the preparation of the manuscript would have been a burden indeed. To my wife Margaret, for her invaluable assistance as wise counselor, critic, and careful proofreader, I owe an unpayable debt.

DAVID A. MacLENNAN

Pompano Beach, Florida

## "What child is this?"

TEXT: "*. . . you will name him Jesus—for he will save his people from their sins*" (*Matthew* 1:21, T.E.V.). "*. . . a leader to be the shepherd of my people Israel*" (*Matthew* 2:6, N.E.B.). "*. . . a voice from heaven was heard saying, 'This is my Son, my Beloved* [*or my only Son*], *on whom my favour rests'* " (*Matthew* 3:17, N.E.B.). "*Thomas said, 'My Lord and my God!'* " (*John* 20:28, N.E.B.). "*He reflects the glory of God and bears the very stamp of his nature, upholding the universe by his word of power*" (*Hebrews* 1:3, R.S.V.).

Many of the best-loved Christmas carols and hymns and songs, are as the shocked secularized woman said complainingly, "distressingly theological." One carol sung to the tune "Greensleeves" asks a basic question: "What child is this, who, laid to rest, / On Mary's lap is sleeping? / Whom angels greet with anthems sweet, / While shepherds watch are keeping?" The author answers with the church in all its branches when the church has repeated its central affirmation: "This, this is Christ the King, / Whom shepherds guard and angels sing."

1) At Christmas our Christology must be showing. Taking a few of the answers to the question found in the New Testament, we can help ourselves and our companions on the Bethlehem road to review the meanings of Jesus of Nazareth. We remind ourselves that "Jesus" is the Latinized form of the Hebrew "Joshua," meaning "God will save." So Matthew 1:21. "Christ" is not his family name as "Jones" is of our friend John Jones, but the Greek for the Hebrew "Messiah" signifying the anointed one. He is the Christ, the anointed of God to be the savior or deliverer of all who confide in him. (2) He is the leader as well as Lord, the shepherd of his people Israel and of the new Israel, his church. (3) He is God's loved Son in a sense myste-

rious, unique, and meaningful. "He is the image of his father!" we exclaim when we see a young boy whose resemblance to his parent is striking. It is so with this Son of God's love whose coming we hail at this season.

4) He is also authentically, completely human as Luke 2:52 attests and assumes, and many another scriptural reference. He was no demigod masquerading as a man. He knew, as we know, fatigue, disappointment, tears, sweat, and, at least momentarily, black despair (on the cross). We may prefer to express our views and the church's views of Christ as "the man for others," "the victim," "the celebrant."*

5) Jesus is certainly our eternal contemporary, present in his body the church, walking every street and highway. A five-year-old boy on his first train ride entered a tunnel. Blackness was followed by daylight and the swift changes evoked this cry from the boy: "It's tomorrow today!" Men and women and boys and girls who join the group around the manger where Christ was laid find it always is like that "in Christ."

*The King of kings salvation brings,*
*Let loving hearts enthrone him.*

## Christmas protocol

TEXT: (*Matthew 2:6; Mark 9:35–36, T.E.V.*)

"Protocol" is a word we owe to the French although the Greeks had the original word for it. It means "the formulary of the etiquette to be observed by the head of state in official ceremonies, etc." (*Shorter Oxford English Dictionary*). Many governments have a department or office of protocol to draw up the order of seating guests at state banquets and so forth. Even at Christmas, celebrating the arrival on this planet of One who is hailed at least in scripture and the church's praises as "King of kings and Lord of lords," and who chose the small and weak things of this world to confound the great and powerful, protocol is observed at parties and feasts.

1) The church itself has not learned the true Christmas protocol. In an old New England church at least two hundred

* See *Jesus Our Contemporary*, by Geoffrey Ainger (New York: The Seabury Press, Inc., 1967).

years ago the order of seating in the sanctuary was as follows: "First, dignity of descent; Second, place or public office; Third, pious disposition; Fourth, estate; Last, peculiar serviceableness of any kind." We smile at such unchristian snobbishness, but could we be guilty of something equally foreign to the life, teaching, example, and words of our Lord? Do we give most attention to the wealthy, the influential, the "power structure" representatives? A Frenchman said that Christianity is "the religion of all poor devils." Of course this does not exclude those rich in money; they may be "poor devils" too.

2) Christmas shatters the protocol of which the old New England church list is an example. Even despised, commonplace, "slow" little Bethlehem is more important than Washington, Ottawa, London, Paris, Bonn, Moscow, or Peking. What is the Christmas protocol? Shepherds and humble folk, then the Wise Men. The honest seeker, the sinner who is genuinely sorry, the humble, the "open," the "poor in spirit." Well known is the true story of a famous Scottish professor of Hebrew who as an elder in his kirk distributed the elements of the Lord's Supper. When he came to a young woman who had deep guilt feelings, she hung her head and declined to take the bread and the cup. Whispered the old saint, whom students affectionately called "Rabbi" Duncan: "Tak' it, lassie, tak' it; it's for sinners." Christ is for the least, the lowest, the last, and (it is more than labored alliteration) the lost.

3) You and I may not be on the President's list to receive his personal Christmas greeting. Something infinitely better and life-changing is offered to us: the invitation of the Lord Jesus Christ. He considers the world's "greatest" those who are last in the world's ratings but first in service to God and their fellow souls. A little child grown to maturity insists that the childlike in wonder, trust, and love shall be first.

## Good grief!

TEXT: " '*Happy are those who mourn: / God will comfort them!*' " (*Matthew 5:4, T.E.V.*).

Good grief! Unless the words are an exclamation of surprise or consternation ("Good grief, Charlie Brown!" in the "Peanuts" cartoons), they do not make sense. It is like saying "peaceful war," or "ugly beauty," or "heavenly hell." Can there be such a thing as "good" grief, such persons as "happy" mourners? Jesus said there is good grief and his followers are happy mourners when sorrow strikes. If ever there was a paradox—a statement seemingly self-contradictory and absurd though essentially true—it is this second beatitude. The world says, "Enjoy! enjoy" and Christ says, "Grieve."

1) Our Lord would be among the first to say that there is bad grief. It is the grief that is self-centered, that regards bereavement or some other deprivation of one loved as a diabolical assault. It is the grief that sorrows without hope. Bad grief is what keeps some persons out of the community long after the hurt should have been healed.

2) Good grief is sorrow for the sorrows and tragedies and deprivations of others. It is the sincere sympathy extended to someone in a dark valley. It expresses itself in little acts of kindness when another person or an entire group undergoes severe trials. It is the strong handclasp, the touch on the shoulder, which says more than words. "O the bliss of those who mourn for others and with others who are grieving!"

3) Good grief is sorrow for the sins and moral failures of others. William Barclay and other biblical scholars incline to think that this is the deep meaning of the beatitude. Is there not a kind of strange joy which comes to the soul who knows heartbreak over the world's misery and lends the stubborn ounces of his weight to alleviate it? William Wilberforce, nineteenth-century British reformer and valiant disciple of Christ, sought the freedom of British slaves without resort to war. In the House of Commons he summoned the whole nation to rid itself of this foul blot upon its name and record. "I mean not to accuse anyone," he said, "but to take the shame upon myself in common with the whole Parliament of Great Britain for having the horrid trade carried on under our authority. We are all guilty." In the United States, when a rising young politician named Theodore Roosevelt read a scorching exposure of the poverty in the slums of cities written by Jacob Riis, the latter found a note under his door one day. It read: "Dear Mr. Riis, I have read your book and have come to offer my help." Happy are such mourners over the conditions which degrade and injure God's children.

4) Good grief is also sorrow experienced for our own sins. Sin is not trivial, nor is it a morbid feeling devised by those who have a vested interest in dispensing assurances of pardon. When we see what our sins have done to those we love, have

done to the heart of God as we know that heart in the living Christ, we too say with the publican in Jesus' parable: "God, be merciful to me a sinner." Penitence is the first step in the Christian life and penitence is sorrow for our sins. We feel this deeply when we think of the crucifixion of the fairest and best, even Jesus our Lord. It is then that we realize that sin such as ours can smash the loveliest and most loving life on a cross. Then comes the joy of forgiveness (see Psalm 51:17, R.S.V.).

5) Good grief is the grief for mourning the death or other form of loss of one dear to us. It is the sorrow which should issue in tears. In the Greek, the word translated "mourn" is associated with tears. How wrong has been the teaching given to boys that to cry is to act like a "sissy." Grief must work itself out and through. "Jesus wept," says the gospel record of his friend Lazarus' death. Yet good grief for one gone through physical death into life's next dimension is the grief which holds fast to hope (see 1 Thessalonians 4:13).

*Rockefeller Chapel Sermons* includes a most helpful sermon on this theme by Dr. Granger E. Westberg, who spells out ten stages of grief.*

"Happy are those who mourn: God will comfort them!" said the Lord of life and death. The word "comforted" is the word used to summon to one's side an ally, a helper, a counselor. God treats the Christian sorrower as an honored guest. Happy are those who in their grief turn to Christ, for they shall find in him an ally, a friend, a presence to comfort them and send them on their way better disciples, concerned about Christ's cause in the world.

## Happy are the hated!

TEXT: " '*Happy are those who suffer persecution because they do what God requires: / the Kingdom of heaven belongs to them! / Happy are you when men insult you and mistreat you and tell all kinds of evil lies against you because you are my followers. Rejoice and be glad, because a great reward is kept for you in heaven. This is how men mistreated the prophets who lived before you.*' " (*Matthew 5:10–12,* T.E.V.).

* *Rockefeller Chapel Sermons of Recent Years,* ed. D. E. Smucker (Chicago: University of Chicago Press, 1967), pp. 178–87.

## [16] **Happy are the hated!**

1) To be "tremendously glad" when we are blamed and ill-treated seems to be the mark of a sick personality. The psychologists have a word for those who enjoy receiving punishment: masochists. Yet here is Jesus saying, as J. B. Phillips translates the words, "what happiness will be yours when people blame you and ill-treat you and say all kinds of slanderous things against you for my sake!"

The last three words in that sentence give the key. When we are hated for Jesus' sake, hated and ill-treated because we are trying to follow him in our relationships, in a task which we know is required of obedient disciples, then we can be glad. Obviously, we need to be sure that what has aroused fierce opposition and even hatred is part of Christ's mission in our time. Scholars point out that before the end of the first century of the Christian era the word for "witness" and the word for "martyr" had become the same Greek word. To follow Christ is to carry a cross. As a seventeenth-century saint named Samuel Rutherford said, "If you have not got a cross you have not got Christ, for it is the first of his gifts" (see Matthew 16:24).

2) In North America, informed observers of our social scene are sure that Christians, both white and black, will experience continued and mounting violence before the war against poverty and other injustice is won. In his devotional meditations on the famous prayer of St. Francis of Assisi, the South African Christian leader Alan Paton devotes a chapter to this uncomfortable possibility. The prayer is the one beginning, "Lord, make me an instrument of thy peace." When Mr. Paton comes to the final petition—"it is in dying that we are born again to eternal life"—he cites the violence of the long, hot summer of 1967.* He asks, "Why is there all this depth of hatred?" He cites historic causes beginning with the slavery of centuries ago. Realistically, Mr. Paton states that we shall have to endure hatred while we are building a society in which there will be justice and freedom and opportunity for all. "While we are building it we are going to be hated, cursed, stoned, shot at, perhaps even killed, by some of the very people for whom we are building it." But the task must be undertaken.

3) We must undertake the task and accept the misunderstanding and try to realize why we are opposed and even hated.

* *Instrument of Thy Peace* (New York: The Seabury Press, Inc., 1967), p. 111.

Mr. Paton finds inspiration in recalling the 1940 bombing of London, England. London was burning, and Churchill called every Londoner to move from basements to roofs to do his share to extinguish the fires. In the face of possible total estrangement between black and white, each of us "must ask to be made an instrument of God's peace, so that one more healing stream may flow into the river of hate."

This is the way our Lord went. Can we do other than follow him? (1 Peter 4:13–16). Indeed, as St. Paul saw with deep insight, when we meet hatred without violence, hatred or cowardice, we help to complete the total of Christ's sufferings (Colossians 1:24).

## Publicity and privacy

TEXT: ". . . *your light must shine before people, so that they will see the good things you do and give praise to your Father in heaven.*" (*Matthew* 5:16, T.E.V.) "*Be careful not to perform your religious duties in public so that people will see what you do. If you do these things publicly you will not have a reward from your Father in heaven*" (*Matthew* 6:1).

How can we publicize our faith and goodness, and at the same time avoid publicity in being Christian? Did Jesus advocate two mutually contradictory practices? No, for our Lord advocates living above the average in society, not to gain prestige for ourselves or a reputation for personal virtue, but to remind observers of the divine source of all that is good. In our own time a perceptive non-Christian scholar declared, "For the sake of Jesus!' Of what noble lives and gracious deeds has this not been the motive and the explanation!" In the paradox of these two verses, Christ teaches that we must not separate the inwardness of our faith from the "practical Christianity" so desperately needed. Also, he underlines the necessity of cultivating the spiritual presence of the One we serve. In modern jargon, "output" requires "input." Our Lord himself withdrew from the crowd to practice the presence of the Father in order to return to the crowd better equipped to meet their needs.

[18]

## "Are you running with me, Jesus?"

TEXT: (*Matthew 6:5–8, T.E.V.*).

It is an unusual question. To some reverent souls it sounds flippant, even vulgar. It is neither. The question is the title of a book* of unconventional prayers written by an unconventional servant of Christ, the Reverend Malcolm Boyd, Episcopal priest, now field representative of his church's Society for Cultural and Racial Unity.

In this book Boyd is not patronizingly familiar with our Lord; no man could pray directly to Jesus without a high view of Christ. (1) These prayers rebuke our own sporadic, often formal private prayer practice. To read such prayers is to realize that personal prayer and public worship are two essential sources of Christian behavior and Christian social action. Jesus commanded that we pray and pray sincerely and privately as well as worship in spirit and reality. We are not to pile up "meaningless phrases," our Lord said. So Matthew reports in this sixth chapter. (2) Prayer must be offered to the God we know in Jesus Christ. If, as Boyd acknowledges, our prayer life is "neither very respectable nor quite correct," keep the Christlike Father steadily in mind. He is the God of unlimited love, unfailing compassion, untiring caring. (3) When we pray we must remember that nothing is too small or too great or too "daily" to pray about. As Thomas Aquinas said, it is legitimate to pray to God for anything it is legitimate to ask God for. So we bring to God: our adoring love for his undeserved patience and goodness; our concerns about our own impatience in traffic or anywhere else; the deviates we may know or know about; the Negro who has had his manhood attacked; the children and old people in life-denying slums; Vietnam and Santo Domingo; the church in its institutional forms. (4) We are to pray asking not only are we running with Jesus, but also whether Jesus can "run" with us. Are we going his way in our family, work, play, community relationships, and activities? (5) We should pray with confidence. God answers prayer. We have the word of the highest spiritual authority for it: see Matthew 18:19, 20. God answers; sometimes "Yes," at other times "No," and sometimes "Wait." Always God answers *us,* meets the need he knows may

* *Are You Running with Me, Jesus?* (New York: Holt, Rinehart & Winston, Inc., 1965).

be deeper than the need we voice. So the writer of Psalm 138:3 testified: "On the day I called, thou didst answer me, my strength of soul thou didst increase" (R.S.V.).

## How to get what you need through prayer

TEXT: "*In your prayers do not use a lot of words, as the pagans do, who think that God will hear them because of their long prayers. Do not be like them; your Father already knows what you need before you ask him. This is the way you should pray: 'Our Father in heaven: May your name be kept holy . . .'*" (*Matthew 6:7–9, T.E.V.*).

1) How to get what you *want* through prayer? No; no one can promise that, if only because what we want may be wrong for us to receive, contrary to what is God's will for his human children. Christian faith teaches that we may get what we *need,* because God wants us to have what we need for a full, satisfying, abundant life. But through prayer? Your experience with prayer may lead you to doubt its efficacy. A useful illustration will be found in the opening of George A. Buttrick's sermon on prayer in *Sermons Preached in a University Church.**

We pray, as William James said, because we simply cannot help praying. But why "Keep on praying and never lose heart . . ." as Jesus said we should (Luke 18:1, N.E.B.)? Why pray when, as Jesus said, our heavenly Father knows what we need before we tell him? Because even a human parent who loves and forgives a child who has done wrong cannot give his love and pardon so that the child can experience it until the child comes and asks for forgiveness and to be taken back again into the family love. Immediately after Jesus affirms the Father's knowledge of our needs, he gives the word: "This is the way you should pray: . . ." Then follows what we should call "the disciples' prayer," the model or pattern prayer. It was as if his first followers said, "Teach us the technique of prayer." If prayer is natural and spiritual why bother with a technique? Because we are finite beings, and the most natural things, such as breathing, are better for knowing how to do them correctly.

2) We obtain what we need when we pray holding the highest concept of God we can picture. Jesus told us to say

* (Nashville: Abingdon Press, 1959), pp. 131–32.

"Our Father in heaven." His favorite word for God was *Abba.* New Testament scholars tell us it was the favorite word of a Jewish child for his father when the child loved his parent dearly. Its nearest equivalent in English is "daddy." Of course it is grotesque to address God as "Daddy," but the word does convey the intimate, unfailingly loving relationship (Mark 14:36; Romans 8:15).

3) Next, we are to pray honestly. Said blunt Martin Luther, "Don't lie to God." We often do. We ask for graces and gifts which would embarrass us greatly if we received them. St. Augustine was at least honest when he prayed, "Make me pure, but not yet!"

4) Pray definitely. Ask for specific blessings. Ask on behalf of specified persons.

5) Pray naturally. There is much that can be said for the use of the august and elegant Elizabethan English of the prayer book and the King James Version of the Bible in liturgical services. Many of us are traditionalists in public prayer. Nevertheless, the "you" and "your" of a youngster's prayers are natural and often more real to the person using them than the "thou" and "thy" and "wast" of the older forms.

6) Pray with your petitions and intercessions "screened" through the mind and spirit of Christ. We are to pray "through Jesus Christ our Lord" not only in the sense of Christ being our mediator, but because we must pray only for such things as we can imagine Christ himself asking God to give and do. To pray that it will not rain on our picnic or parade may be the acme of selfishness; farmers may need rain desperately to save their crops to feed the world's hungry. To pray for a miracle to be worked when we have failed to do our homework is contrary to the laws of the universe and the teaching of Christ. We can pray, "Let me face this ordeal, this examination, this test, this situation, with calmness and courage." Our prayer will be answered. We get what we need through prayer when we make the effort with God's help to make our prayer come true. "This is the way you should pray: . . ."

## Spiritual cosmetics

TEXT: " '*And when you fast, do not put on a sad face like the show-offs do. They go around with a hungry look so that everybody will be sure to see that they are fasting.*

*Remember this! They have already been paid in full'* "
(*Matthew 6:16, T.E.V.*).

1) Disfigured faces can be greatly improved by plastic surgery. Dismal faces can be greatly improved by the joy of Christ. Even today, when we no longer believe that cheerfulness is to be suspected, at least among the godly, too many Christians look unhappy, depressed, sad. In an earlier generation it may have been even more common. One "help wanted" advertisement for a domestic ended with the phrase that the applicant should be "a Christian," and then added, "cheerful, if possible."

Years ago, an Oxford, England, scholar and Christian philosopher named L. P. Jacks wrote a provocative essay on what he called "The Lost Radiance of the Christian Religion."* Jesus our Lord asks us when we fast—or practice the equivalent in self-denial—that we do not do it as play actors might do, by disfiguring our faces. ". . . wash your face and comb your hair . . ." he urged (verse 17). In other words, apply some spiritual make-up.

Naturally we grow weary of the habitually happy-faced person. Life can be grim, tragic: "there is a time to weep, and a time to laugh," as Ecclesiastes said. But how impressive it is, in a world where there are too many unnecessary crosses and crises, to make contact with a radiant soul! After his lamented early death, Archbishop of Canterbury William Temple was paid a memorable tribute by a workingman in England. This man said, "We shall miss him, for he was such a jolly man." William Temple was no Pollyanna, no Micawber; he knew the tragic side of life and he labored diligently to try to right wrongs and establish the right. Nevertheless, his inward companionship with Christ, his fellowship with Christ's people—saints and sinners alike—made him one of the Lord's merry men.

2) As we leave God's house today will we look any different to an observant "outsider"? An overseas writer reminds us that our faces are among the most revealing parts of our bodies. Haven't we read or said such phrases as "his face dropped," or "her face lit up," or "his face looked like the wrath of God"? But we are Christ's, affirms the Apostle Paul, and Christ's is God's. Therefore, all things are ours; all things that really matter. Lift up your hearts! Let your face light up with

* (New York: George H. Doran Company, 1924).

what Jesus called his joy. "Rejoice in the Lord always," and let others see that we do.

## Sticking to nature and the New Testament

TEXT: "'*And why worry about clothes? Look how the wild flowers grow: they do not work or make clothes for themselves*'" (*Matthew 6:28, T.E.V.*).

Halford E. Luccock used to say that Jesus was not crucified because he said, "Consider the lilies of the field, how they grow," but because he said, "Consider the scribes and Pharisees, how they steal." The oversimplification may be pardoned; stealing is not confined to money and property, and, when caught at it, the thieves incline to strike out violently.

At springtime we may well emulate the Lord of life and give some attention to the lilies of the field and the world of nature they represent. With increasing urbanization of what was once truly rural living, it is salutary to remember that Jesus was a country boy. He was not bred amid the streets and alleys of a city. Whenever the pressures of his public ministry pushed down his spirit he took to the hills, to the lake, to the open sky.

Consider, too, that this preacher of the truth that sets men free used illustrations almost exclusively from what we call nature—from farmers planting crops, shepherds tending their sheep, vineyard workers on their jobs, tiny mustard seeds growing to impressive-size shrubs; from foxes, wolves, hens, swine, the camel, the donkey, the birds—including the sparrow whose funeral God himself attended. Contrast Jesus' use of God's fair and sometimes frightening world of nature with the Apostle Paul's silence about it. City born and city bred, Paul would feel as lonely as a boy shipped for the first time from crowded Manhattan to a New England summer camp far from any town.

What did Jesus perceive and emphasize in "our Father's world"? British preacher G. T. Bellhouse provided a threefold answer: Jesus was always conscious of (1) "the wonder and mystery of nature"; (2) the "reliability, regularity, and responsiveness" of nature; (3) the peacefulness of nature, even when nature produces and exhibits fierce turbulence and terrific storms.*

* *Bread from Heaven* by G. T. Bellhouse (London: The Epworth Press, 1963), pp. 70–72.

Under the first heading, you may think of our Lord's comments about the secrecy of plant growth, of the mysterious blowing of the wind. The great naturalists, the true scientists, have been reverent men and women. Under (2) the preacher will cite Jesus' words about the dependability of nature. Men do not gather grapes from thorns or figs from thistles. Even when a seed seems to die, give it—and God—time, and you will have a harvest. May this quiet, mysterious growth not have been a source of the Lord's own patience when his first followers were so slow of heart to believe? Something there is in this mysterious universe that responds to faith, to love, to Christ-like goodness.

Under (3) the seventh chapter of Matthew will be relevant. "Consider the lilies of the field" which in the Palestine of Jesus' time, as in our time in Jordan and Israel, are far from frail and fragile hothouse blooms. The lilies send down their roots without fanfare or noise and lift their heads to sun and rain. What a contrast to our frenetic, often frenzied fussing. Even the pilot of a bomber can learn to fly relaxed. Why cannot we who are guarded and guided by the divine wisdom, love and power, live with peace at the center? Dr. Edward Wilson, famous scientist and radiant Christian, who perished on the Antarctic expedition of Captain Robert F. Scott, wrote: "So long as I have stuck to Nature and the New Testament, I have only got happier and happier every day." With Christ we are never blind to nature "red in tooth and claw"; we are also aware of God's world of wonder, purpose, peace.

## The Christian cure of worry

TEXT: " '*So do not worry about tomorrow; it will have enough worries of its own. There is no need to add to the troubles each day brings*' " (*Matthew 6:34, T.E.V.*).

Some persons do not worry enough. Blithely they ignore serious causes for anxiety in their own families, communities, world. Creative worry averts grave crises in the domestic, financial, and political worlds. Most of us, including intelligent Christians, worry too much because we worry about the wrong matters. Jesus Christ was no passive quietist. Nevertheless, much of his recorded teaching and his own example of serenity in the midst of a turbulent society emphasize that the wrong kind of worry is a sin. It may not be the greatest sin, but it is one of the most disabling sins. It paralyzes action, tears us into tatters emotionally, contributes to hypertension, and is a factor in causing ulcers. One doctor observed that the incidence of ulcers among certain types of men is related directly to the rise and fall of the stock market.

Jesus never urged us to resolve, "I will NOT worry!" He knew that we must replace anxiety with trust in the God whose providential care of the least of his creation was evident to him. How to carry out our Lord's instruction "So do not worry . . ."? Wise counselors (beginning with James Gordon Gilkey many years ago) are sure that a threefold formula, deceptively simple, holds the key. From the sayings of Jesus, from his own practice, we may find support for these directives.

1) First, limit the load of worries. We can do this by distinguishing between the baseless anxieties and those which have foundation. Some worries should be removed from a Christian's list. These include anxieties about past decisions, about which even God can do nothing except to forgive us our part in the wrong choices, and in the sins of the yesterdays. Among others which we can do nothing about are the events which will occur regardless of our planning and control. Recall the person who analyzed his worries and learned that only eight percent were legitimate and that about these God's Spirit of wisdom and power could help him do much. When we worry about other people's criticisms of us and our actions, it is good to remember who said, "How terrible when all men speak well of you . . ." (Luke 6:26, R.S.V.). Also, it is sound sense to remind ourselves that the most perfect person who ever lived did not please everybody.

2) The second wisdom about life which Christ illumines and confirms is this: break up the load of anxieties. Jesus lived a busy, crowded life. But he was never hectic. "Are there not twelve hours in the day?" he asked (John 11:9, R.S.V.). "Your Father in heaven knows that you need all these things" (Matthew 6:32). "These things" referred to necessities about which we often fret and fume. You and I can manage a single day, a single hour, one minute. "Let the day's own trouble be sufficient for the day" (Matthew 6:34, R.S.V.).

3) The third guideline is: share the load. With whom? With God; he loves the burden. The writer of the First Letter of Peter has a wonderful word: "Cast all your anxieties on him, for he cares about you" (1 Peter 5:7, R.S.V.). Over a century ago,

a young man dedicated himself to a Christian career. As he began his diary he wrote his expression of confidence that God would guide him. His last entry, written in a trembling hand, is worth remembering. This veteran disciple of Christ summed up his life: "Led by his Spirit all the way."

## "Unbelievably detailed"

TEXT: " '*You can buy two sparrows for a penny; yet not a single one of them falls to the ground without your Father's consent. As for you, even the hairs of your head have all been counted. So do not be afraid: you are worth much more than sparrows!*' " (*Matthew 10:29–31, T.E.V.*).

"Unbelievably detailed." What is? God's fatherly love. So says New Testament scholar Professor William Barclay in his studies in the Lord's Prayer. Our greatest authority on God—Jesus Christ—assures us that God cares for all his children with a love that never fails or forgets or forsakes. He loves us, as Augustine and many another Christian has said, as if each of us were the only child in his great family. God's love, taught by Jesus, demonstrated by Jesus' dying and his undying love, is far from the kind of love voiced by Lucy to "good ol' Charlie Brown" in the cartoon strip, "Peanuts." You may recall that she said: "I love humanity! It's people that I can't stand!" God's love embraces the entire creation. You name it and God loves it or him or her. Nevertheless, Dr. Barclay is right: "The wonderful thing about this fatherhood of God is that it is not only universal, as wide as the world, it is *unbelievably detailed.*"

This is the meaning of Jesus' saying, "Two sparrows sell for a penny, don't they? Yet not a single sparrow falls to the ground without your Father's knowledge." Luke reports the saying differently but the same point is made: "Yet not a single one of them is forgotten by God" (Luke 12:6).

In Palestine, when you bought two pennies' worth of sparrows you got not four but five sparrows; the dealer threw an extra one in. They were so cheap as to be almost worthless. But God, says Jesus, cares even about the fifth sparrow, the one that was valueless to the salesman. Surely we can regain a sense of our true worth, of the true worth of the least, the lowest, the so-called "lost."

1) Everyone matters to God.* Christian psychiatrist Dr. Paul Tournier relates the story of a girl, youngest in a large family, whose deep illness could be traced to hearing her father say of her, "We could well have done without that one!" Our Heavenly Father could never say that of the most difficult of his children.

2) Every time we fall to the ground, like a sparrow exhausted or hurt, God sees us and cares. Always God's love, healing, help are present even when we do not recognize the divine source. He uses human agents and instruments. He moves within our minds and spirits to inspire hope and courage.

3) We can confide ourselves, our loved ones, our community, and the cause of Christ to this guiding and sheltering providence and this "unbelievably detailed" love.

4) "If God so loved us, we must also love one another." Where? When? How?

## Is this the one?

TEXT: (*Matthew 11:2–6, T.E.V.*).

1) It was a crucial question when John the Baptist asked it. It is a crucial question now. Imagine a grand jury consisting of all sorts and conditions of men and women: intellectuals, the little people, racists, and fighters for social justice—rebels with and without a cause. Jesus of Nazareth confronts them, and they ask: "Is this the one?" "Are you the one who is to come, or are we to expect some other?" After all, John had preached "the kingdom of heaven is at hand!" and now he languishes in one of Herod's dungeons. He had been attracted to his cousin, but Jesus had fallen far short of expectations. He was no aggressive deliverer, no majestic and severe Messiah quickly smashing evil. In our time men and women who rarely use biblical categories know they need a deliverer, a Lord and leader, an interpreter of this ambiguous life. Is Christ the one? After all, nearly 2,000 years have come and gone since that birth in a stable-cave, those brief years of teaching, healing, proclamation of God's rule and realm. Look at the world! In "Advice from a Mil-

* See A *Doctor's Casebook in the Light of the Bible,* by Paul Tournier (New York: Harper & Row, Publishers, 1960), p. 146.

lionaire Publisher,"* John Hay Whitney writes, "America has enormous power to lead, but no one seems to have enormous will to follow. . . . modern American man, affluent beyond . . . Croesus but not understanding the economics of it . . . Mobile beyond . . . any previous people . . . but not really sure where he wants to go." Add the so-called "new morality" which in personal relationships sometimes resembles that of an unsupervised barnyard. In high places, middle places, and low corruption continues. Where does this Jesus Christ come in?

2) When John's embassy put the question to Jesus, he answered clear and strong. You are to judge for yourselves, he said; let the facts speak. Jesus' language may have reminded John of Isaiah's description of the effects of the mission of the Servant of the Lord (Isaiah 61). Jesus seemed to say that God takes no shortcuts. His way of redemptive love joined with justice offers no quick cure like some headache tablet dispenses. Yet miracles of healing, of mercy, of brotherhood follow the action of this Lord. "Go and tell John what you hear and see." (a) *The blind recover their sight.* Spiritual companionship with the living Christ takes the film from our eyes. We are able to see ourselves, our fellow men, the divine reality with whom we have to do. (b) *The lame walk.* Who doesn't know what it is to start out briskly on the road of living and slowly or suddenly go lame? With all our resourcefulness, we are not strong enough to keep on the road of the good life. We keep stumbling. Then Christ comes, like a great orthopedic surgeon, and we are whole again. (c) *The lepers are cleansed.* Few moderns would speak of themselves as did the valiant Father Damien when he contracted the dread physical disease from those he served: "We lepers." But we know this twist in human nature, this deep-seated malaise that defies every known therapy. Christ is what God does for us when we need forgiveness, acceptance, and a new life. (d) *The deaf hear.* When conscience speaks and we do not hear, Christ comes to restore our hearing. He makes us hear the thrilling music of the Spirit's voice; he makes us hear also the still sad music of rejected, despairing, imprisoned humanity. (e) *The dead are raised to life again.* A London music-hall comedian sang of one who was "dead but he won't fall down." Not comic but tragic when we go through the motions of living but

* *Saturday Review,* December 12, 1964, pp. 71–73.

lack zest, vitality, direction. Eternal life here and now as well as hereafter and forever is life from a great depth of being, and it is life abundant. (f) *The poor are hearing the good news.* Long before our "war on poverty," Christ launched his offensive against poverty of every kind. Economic necessities must be made available to all, but after this program is operating well, many still will live a marginal spiritual life. No one is truly rich until he knows he is loved and can and does love in return. This is why in Lent we make spiritual pilgrimage with Christ and to Christ as he moves toward Calvary and death. Christ on the Cross is God speaking to us: "You are loved so much. Go and tell John what you see and hear."

## Fear, facts, and faith

TEXT: (*Matthew 11:2–10, T.E.V.*).

In many branches of the church a Sunday near Christmas is used to tell the story of the amazing forerunner, pathfinder, and cousin of Jesus we know as John the Baptizer. In today's scripture we have what television and motion picture producers might call a "montage." We are shown this rugged evangelist of the Jordan country in prison, but desperately concerned to know if Jesus of Nazareth was the one whose coming John had announced. He was afraid, as sometimes in our dark moods we may be afraid, that Jesus may not be the one to set the people free.

1) *Fear was expressed.* "Are you the one who was to come or are we to look for somebody else?" (Matthew 11:3, J.B.P.). It is good to verbalize our fears or—as psychologists sometimes say—to "exteriorize" them. It is not Christian to repress our doubts and questions.

2) *Facts were made known.* "Jesus answered, 'Go and tell John what you hear and see: The blind recover their sight, the lame walk, the lepers are made clean, the deaf hear, the dead are raised to life, the poor are hearing the good news—and happy is the man who does not find me a stumbling-block' " (Matthew 11:4–6, N.E.B.). When you go where Christ's action is, action of men and women and boys and girls who are "in Christ," you see the unmistakable proofs of the reality of Christ as Savior, Lord, and Life Giver. The "antiestablishment kick"

would lose much of its power if men and women would see the Christian church reproducing the deeds of Christ. In many urban areas, in many suburbs, in many nations, Christ is at work through Christians.

3) *Faith was invited.* J. B. Phillips renders Jesus' final words to John: "And happy is the man who never loses his faith in me" (verse 5). If you have expressed your fear, and faced the facts of Christ's truth and power to transform life, then give him your loyalty, your trust, your faith. Join that legion of the committed for whom our Lord gave thanks: "O Father, Lord of heaven and earth! I thank you because you have shown to the unlearned what you have hidden from the wise and learned" (Matthew 11:25, T.E.V.).

## "We're not interested"

TEXT: *"Now, to what can I compare the people of this day? They are like children sitting in the market place. One group shouts to the other, 'We played wedding music for you, but you would not dance! We sang funeral songs, but you would not cry!' " (Matthew 11:2–19. Text verses 16–17, T.E.V.).*

1) "We're not interested" is what the generation to which Jesus referred responded to the spiritual challenge of both John the Baptist and Jesus the Christ. This little parable shows how different John and Jesus were, and it also shows clearly that both were widely rejected. In a clever manner people excused themselves for their refusal to accept their spiritual responsibility. John, they said, was too stern and demanding; Jesus too lax and unrealistic in preaching love to men of all sorts. They would have neither the asceticism of John nor the love of Jesus. In modern idiom, Jesus' fellow countrymen preferred to "play it cool," taking no sides.

2) Today there is widespread patronage of religion, at least in America, but increasing numbers of citizens enjoy religion less. For the relatively few who are antiestablishment there are many who simply do not come to church. Dietrich Bonhoeffer described their thinking this way, "more goes on in the cinema, it is really more interesting."* If the movies are not today's preferred alternative, television or the country

* *No Rusty Swords* (New York: Harper & Row, Publishers, 1965), p. 154.

cottage or the weekend sports activity may be. Bonhoeffer thought that God may be teaching these people to live without him. These are those who if they have any Christianity have the "religionless" kind.

3) Jesus put the blame squarely on ". . . the people of this day . . ." Can we do so until we are sure that we present the claims of Christ and his church with something of the fervor and responsibility of John the Baptist and the joy and caring of Christ? But let's face it, many of us are petulant Christians who need to be faced with our irresponsibility. Christianity could disappear in a generation if every nominal Christian regressed into infantile irresponsibility.

## The best things in life are free?

TEXT: (*Matthew 13:44–45, T.E.V.*).

Perennial showman Jack Benny once spoke of his gang. These are his contemporaries who have been thirty-nine for the last twenty or thirty years. He said they are known as the Ovaltine àgo-goes, and their music is that of Lawrence Welk records. When these estimable citizens were in the 1930s there was a popular song which celebrated the claim that "The best things in life are free." Is this true or false? From Christian perspective the answer must be, "True *and* false."

1) In a profound sense the best things of life are free. "What is there," asks the Apostle, "that you have not received?" All is of grace. By grace we are saved by faith, "and this is not your own doing, but God's gift." We did not pay for our birth into the world. Nor can we pay for the love which we have experienced since our arrival. As the prayer of General Thanksgiving puts it, "we give humble and hearty thanks for our creation, preservation, and all the blessings of this life." We do not send a check to cover the cost. "And above all," continues the prayer, "for the redemption of the world by our Lord Jesus Christ." Life, love, freedom, friendship, our eternal hope —all these are free. We can but make grateful response, which is what is meant by Christian stewardship of time, talent, treasure.

2) On the other side of this truth is what appears to be its opposite. Life's best things include those which are not free.

"You were bought with a price," flatly declares the New Testament. "There is no redemption without the shedding of blood." This is true whether our redemption is thought of in terms of deliverance from the power of sin and of death, or as deliverance from the tyrannies and injustices of man's contriving in our present society and culture. As a nation our freedom has been paid for again and again and at a terribly high price. Think of Valley Forge, Gettysburg, the Marne, Argonne, Iwo Jima, Salerno, Normandy, Korea. As for the Christian home, is there not a price for its building and continuance? Self-denial, self-discipline, self-control? As for mankind's redemption, is not the Cross the price tag? It cost *that* much, says the God encountered in the Crucified Redeemer.

What we most desire for ourselves and for our children and for our brothers and sisters around the world is not free; it must be paid for in lives laid down, in comforts spurned, in money spent, in dogged and often dull plodding at the tasks of ending poverty, slums, and the indifference and arrogance and greed which perpetuate them.

Dr. Halford E. Luccock told of looking at the cost of miniature globes which a granddaughter wanted. A school supplies catalogue disclosed that an illuminated globe cost twice as much as the unlighted kind. A lighted globe costs twice as much as one without the light of Christ's gospel, life, presence. The alternative is a blackout induced by men refusing to pay the price. Look at the two little parables. Get the point.

## Welcome aboard

TEXT: "*They both got back into the boat, and the wind died down*" (*Matthew 14:32, T.E.V.*).

"Welcome aboard!" is one nautical phrase most landlubbers have used. When a new person joins a firm, a church staff, a club, the greeting rings out. Nineteen centuries ago, a little group of frightened men said this in effect to one they first thought was a ghost. It was Jesus, and their first response to his coming to them through the storm was one of dread. Then, according to the Fourth Gospel account (see John 6), they were delighted to have him climb on board helping the panic-stricken Simon Peter out of the raging waters of that turbulent little inland sea.

1) To rationalize this "nature miracle" seems like wasted effort. Whatever happened, this story did much to strengthen the early church's confidence in their Lord. First, it reminded them of what Psalm 107, verses 23–30 (R.S.V.), sang in memorable words, that God rules his universe, that he can make "the storm be still" and bring any ship of the soul into its desired haven. Second, the story would convince them that Jesus Christ showed himself the unique instrument of this infinitely wise and powerful God.

2) We need to welcome the Lord of life and history aboard our ships. When Pierre Curie was killed in an accident, his wife Marie wrote to a friend: "What do I do now?" When grief strikes, when our little but precious world seems to collapse around us, what do we do? We do not now brashly proclaim that we are captains of our fate. Welcome aboard, Lord. "They both got into the boat, and the wind died down." The British have a colloquialism: "he got his wind up." We know what it means. But let the Master join us, and somehow peace and power return.

3) Welcome aboard, Lord, because we need your love. In our kind of world, with our kind of nature, we need your love, not only to assure us that your love is the greatest force, from which neither life nor death can separate us, but we need your love to help us respond with true love to those we love. Even more, it is the love of Christ in us that enables us to love, in the New Testament sense, those we cannot like. "So they gladly took him aboard" (John 6:21, J.B.P.).

## Do you hate the Cross?

TEXT: "*When the disciples all came together in Galilee, Jesus said to them: 'The Son of Man is about to be handed over to men who will kill him; but on the third day he will be raised to life.' The disciples became very sad*" (*Matthew* 17:22, 23, T.E.V.).

Goethe, the German philosopher and poet, is reported to have said: "There are four things I hate: first, tobacco smoke; second, lice; third, garlic; and fourth, the cross." If ever there was a strange combination of things detested, this must be it. Many twentieth-century persons, including some respectable citizens, hate the cross of Christ. Like some of the early heretics, they prefer to believe that the dear Lord never really dies. But the largest part of the Four Gospels is devoted to Christ's suffering and death. Indeed, we cannot have Christianity without the cross. It may be scandalous to sensitive or sophisticated moderns, but there it is, hard wood, and the grain is red, the cross on which Jesus Christ died.

Why do we hate the cross? (1) Because it seems to us morbid to linger long on the fact of death, and particularly the death of the fairest and best. Evelyn Waugh's satirical novel *The Loved One,** about the California cemetery where death and the dead are never mentioned, appeals to more of us than we may suspect. (2) We may hate the cross because it speaks of sacrifice. Bertrand Russell once fulminated against Christianity because it makes so much of sacrifice. He was sick of hearing about it, he said. But there is no gain except through pain, no life except through death, no redemption even on a humanistic basis without sacrifice. It seems to be a law of life.

3) We may hate the cross of Christ because it makes us face up to our own sin and failure. The cross of Christ reveals the sin of men and women like ourselves as well as the love of God. We may not wish anyone to die for us and for our remaking and rescue, but the fact remains that One has died for us. However we may interpret Christ's death, something was done through it that we and all men needed to have done; something was done there on the cross which we could not do for ourselves. So we sing with the hymn writer, "I take, O cross, thy shadow, for my abiding place" ("Beneath the Cross of Jesus," by Elizabeth C. Clephane). Like the disciples who ". . . became very sad . . ." when Jesus told them of his approaching death (Matthew 17:23), we may regret deeply that ours is the kind of world and we are the kind of people who can be saved only by Christ's death, but now we ". . . boast only of the cross of our Lord Jesus Christ . . ." (Galatians 6:14).

## Asking the right questions

TEXT: "*I will ask you just one question. . . .*" (*Matthew 21:24, T.E.V.*).

* (Boston: Little, Brown and Company, 1950).

1) More than many generations, ours is one which asks questions. Some are trivial, some are impossible to answer, many are important, and a few relate to life, death, the individual's future, and the world's destiny. Dr. Donald Soper, of the famous Tower Hill open-air forum in London, England, observed some years ago that the Christian church is a magnificent institution for answering questions no one is asking. Unfortunately, this is true in many instances. Preachers and ecclesiastical councils spend time, thought, energy in providing answers to what they deem significant, timely questions, and the majority couldn't care less.

2) If Christians are answering questions nobody is asking, or if we are not providing answers to the real questions, we must help people ask the right questions. Dean John Killinger of Kentucky Southern College, Louisville, tells of an exchange between George Buttrick, when he was preacher at Harvard's Memorial Church, and Archibald MacLeish. After first declining Dr. Buttrick's invitation to conduct morning prayers, MacLeish accepted but made his position clear: "I'm not at all convinced that Christianity has the answers we're looking for—but I do think it has the right questions."*

Think of the "right questions" the Bible asks. Many of them are asked in our time, although often in sharper, less elegant language than scripture employs. These questions include: Who am I? Is there meaning in life? How can I be just as well as loving? Who needs religion? Why get involved with the troubles or needs of others? Why be responsible for anyone other than one's self? Why is Jesus Christ necessary to a working faith? Why not scrap the "old morality"?

3) Here are some questions Jesus might ask of us: Why have you so little faith in God? in your fellow man? in yourself? Why don't you do what is right? Why do you think the Christian basis for action is nonsense in this kind of world? Why doesn't your "religionless Christianity" or "God-is-dead" philosophy give you more joy? The late, beloved Halford E. Luccock had an inimitable sermon (although many have been tempted to imitate him!) on this theme.† Hal was sure that when Jesus asked questions he was "pushing his attack into the opponent's corner, a

* *The Thickness of Glory* by John Killinger (Nashville: Abingdon Press, 1965), pp. 91, 92.

† See *Marching Off the Map* (New York: Harper & Row, Publishers, 1952), p. 114.

strategy of tremendous value, and all too often neglected." When opponents or "outsiders" put their difficult and sometimes damning questions to Christians, we ought to be able to come back as our Lord did: "I will also ask you a question."

4) Jesus Christ—all that we mean when we say "Our Lord Jesus Christ"—is himself the answer as well as the basic question. He does more than answer life's dark questions such as, Why do the innocent suffer? Why are the good not able? Christ gives us enough light on every question to find working solutions, light enough in any dark to walk by, and power for the journey as we follow him.

## Are we wearing the right clothes?

TEXT: "*'Friend, how did you get in here without wedding clothes?' the king asked him*" (*Matthew 22:11–14, T.E.V.*).

Casual living characterizes our society. Most of us find it enjoyable. This is why this little parable, apparently tacked on the longer one of the wedding feast, seems outdated. To some readers it may seem like a kind of editorial insertion; it seems so unlike Jesus to make much of formality in clothes or anything else. But is it outdated and inconsistent with Jesus' views? Even when we are invited to many events to come as we are, we would be reluctant to attend a formal wedding in a sports shirt and Bermuda shorts. Granted, clothes do not make the man or indicate a person's true worth. God, says the scripture (1 Samuel 16:7, R.S.V.) ". . . sees not as man sees; man looks on the outward appearance, but the Lord looks on the heart."

(1) Nevertheless, Jesus told this story for a purpose. Here was a man invited to a royal marriage banquet who did not prepare as he should have done. As was a custom in the East in Jesus' time, the host inspected the guests, "and he saw a man who was not wearing wedding clothes. 'Friend, how did you get in here without wedding clothes?' the king asked him. But the man said nothing." The ushers threw the sloppily dressed guest "outside in the dark." Is Jesus telling us that to enjoy divine hospitality it is not enough to be present, even to participate, without assuming obligations? The apostle Paul insisted that we must not exploit divine grace nor use Christian freedom as an excuse for license.

(2) Are we wearing the right clothes? The question relates not to legalism but to love. What are the right clothes? Bishop Gerald Kennedy reminds us that the right clothes consist of *repentance,* which means we discard completely the clinging robe of sophistication, of false pride, of sin; of *sincerity,* which enables us to be free from any compulsion to pretend.* You must, says the New Testament, *put on Christ,* when you get rid of your old self, . . ." (see Ephesians 4:22–24). It is good to link this requirement with Isaiah 61:10 and with Luke 15:22 where the waiting father ". . . called to his servants: 'Hurry!' he said. 'Bring the best robe and put it on him . . .' " God offers us the new clothes of forgiveness, of acceptance, of newness of life. Let's put them on!

## Shocking!

TEXT: ". . . *the crowds . . . were amazed at his teaching*" (*Matthew 22:33, T.E.V.*).

"Shocking!" This is what many Christians said when they visited the Christian Pavilion at Expo 67, the Canadian world exhibition in Montreal. Kenneth Bagnell, United Church of Canada writer, reported that "the foreign and Canadian press are speculating that it may well be the shock of the entire exhibition." The word "shocking" is used in more than one sense. To some it is shocking in the sense of offensive or revolting. To others it is shocking in the sense of astonishing or astounding. The gospel writers tell us that Jesus Christ had this effect upon followers and bystanders alike. When Jesus "fielded" one of the trickiest questions the Sadducees put to him about a much-married woman and her possible partner in the resurrection, "they were astonished [astounded or shocked] at his teaching."

At Expo 67 many were "shocked" because they found none of the conventional things associated in their minds with the Christian faith. There was no pulpit, no statue or picture of the Lord. "Instead the designer has used completely modern tools, lights, sounds, films, and above all pictures—possibly the most moving collection of pictures ever presented." Expo 67's Christian Pavilion operates on three levels. At every level of

* *The Parables* (New York: Harper & Row, 1960), pp. 143-51.

man's life it is shocking to face honestly what man is, what God had done and is doing to change him, and what man must do with this world because of it.

Like the Pavilion's three levels, consider Christ confronting us on *three levels.* (1) The first level is the normal life, our day-to-day existence. There is beauty, tedium, and the eccentric. Birth, marriage, vocational choice and activity, and death—these, as we say, are normal, "par for the course." Christ says to us, to every man, "Come to me that you may really live." It is a shock to realize we may be just going through the motions of existence and not living from a great depth of being. (2) In life, as in the Christian Pavilion at the now famous exhibition, there is the negative level. This is where the realist descends into the abyss of despair. At Expo 67 there was an almost terrifying motion picture film showing the horrors and cruelties of our history from prize fighting to Hiroshima. Leaving the film, you were then confronted by pictures of a Vietnam grave and of children playing ball, some with one leg or arm missing—war's aftermath.

But, thank God, there is in the human situation, as in the Pavilion, a third level of hope and redemption. God is involved with his human children. If you saw the picture of the child making her way toward the door of a shack, with wild flowers in her arms, you will remember the caption which began, "why seek for me among the dead. I am with you always . . ." Shocking? Astounding? Yes, God's Spirit in the living Christ stabs our spirits broad awake to the reality of evil, to the "everydayness" of existence which ought to be marked by zestfulness, joy, hope and to his action to lift existence to the level of meaningful, redeemed, purposeful life in the death, resurrection and continued presence of Christ with all who put their trust in him. "They were astonished." Many were shocked, offended. "Blessed are you if you are not offended in me," he said. Are we?

## Will the real Christian stand up?

TEXT: (*Matthew 25:31–46, T.E.V.*).

This is the most disturbing story Jesus told. To the sincere Christian who believes that we are justified, accepted, forgiven not by "works" but by our trusting faith in Christ, it comes as a shock to be told something which seems completely contrary. What we have done, or not done, to the least of Christ's brethren—that is decisive. Final judgment will turn upon the fruits—even, it seems, more than upon the roots—of vital faith. More than this shocking teaching is the implication that we shall be judged by the actions we did or did not do, unconsciously. Our Lord never dismissed faith or belief, provided it was genuine and placed in the God whom he knew from first-hand experience and whom he disclosed in his life and death and resurrection. He frequently deplored the lack of adequate faith. This is the test of Christian faith and commitment: what we do or do not do for others. A wise preacher found three simple divisions of this parable: (1) here is something we can all do; (2) here is something we can all do for its own sake; (3) here is something we can all do which turns out to be done to Christ.

## That tore it!

TEXT: *"Then the curtain hanging in the Temple was torn in two, from top to bottom"* (*Matthew 27:51, T.E.V.*). (*See also Mark 15:38, Luke 23:45.*)

In World War II, British soldiers had a slang expression, "That tore it" or "That tears it." It was their way of saying, "It is finished, there is nothing more to be done." All three synoptic gospels report that at the moment Jesus died, the veil or curtain which separated ordinary people from the holy of holies —the inner sanctuary and alter—had been destroyed. Professor James S. Stewart of Edinburgh has a powerful sermon on "The Rending of the Veil." Its substance is included in his Lyman Beecher Lectures on Preaching delivered at Yale University.*

This temple curtain fulfilled a double function: to keep men out of the final mysteries of religion and to shut God in. Superstitious Jews of the time believed there was a mysterious presence behind that curtain. (1) Jesus' death opened the way into the holiest of all, into the heart of God. (2) Jesus' death ended all exclusiveness, segregation, particularism. He opened up the way to the kingdom of God with his life. (3) The death of

* *A Faith to Proclaim* (New York: Charles Scribner's Sons, 1952), pp. 80–84.

Jesus, followed by his resurrection, opened up the way into life eternal. The preacher may wish to look again at the so-called "prayer of the veil" used in some communion services: "O God, who by the Blood of thy dear Son hast consecrated for us a new and living way into the holiest of all. . . ."

## Refracted in the afterglow of Easter

TEXT: "*Suddenly there was a strong earthquake; an angel of the Lord came down from heaven, rolled the stone away, and sat on it*" (*Matthew* 28:2, *T.E.V.*).

Christ's resurrection caused a spiritual, moral, and ethical earthquake in the lives of men and women. Understood and accepted, the risen Lord still shatters the "secure" lives of people. An evangelical scholar in Britain, Dr. E. O. White, is the author of this outline of a topical-textual Christian message: "Refracted in the afterglow of Easter: (1) God was different; (2) the cross was different; (3) Christ was different; (4) the whole world was different." Some earthquake!*

## The Easter "happening"

TEXT: "*He is not here; he has risen, just as he said*" (*Matthew* 28:6, *T.E.V.*).

1) Always the church has claimed that the Resurrection was an actual happening, an event. Ever since the first Easter, Christians have insisted that the evidence pointed to something that happened, something factual, however mysterious. The church points to (a) the tradition of the empty tomb. (Recall the case made out by Frank Morrison in his book *Who Moved the Stone?*)† (b) The post-Resurrection appearances of the living Lord. The New Testament does not resolve the problem of apparent contradictions in the accounts of these appearances. Sometimes Christ eats fish; sometimes he passes through closed doors. (c) The experiences of the early church. Only conviction

* *Sermon Suggestions in Outline* by Dr. E. O. White (London: Pickering and Inglis, Ltd., 1965), pp. 44–47.
† (London: Faber & Faber, 1930).

that Jesus Christ has been raised by God from death can explain the tremendous transformation of defeated, dispirited disciples into daring, triumphant apostles.

2) Nevertheless, in the contemporary sense the resurrection of Christ is a "happening"—it is something you experience, a kind of divine-human "love-in" centered in the unseen but risen and victorious Lord. (a) It is this "happening" which changed the first followers of Jesus mentioned in (c) above. Christ came alive in and among his own. Each once-despondent fisherman and each tearful woman went out to conquer the world in the power of the One whom Paul said lived within his life. (b) This "happening" has recurred in the life of the church ever since. Ours is not a dead hero but a living Lord. He comes to comfort, to challenge, to sustain his people, and he does these amazing things because he is not merely a memory but a reality. (c) We too can testify if Christ has come alive for us and we have "risen with Christ" (see Colossians 3:1–4, particularly in one of the new translations).

## Never underestimate the power of your faith

TEXT: *"Jesus saw how much faith they had, and said to the paralyzed man. 'My son, your sins are forgiven'"* (*Mark 2:5, T.E.V.*).

Sometimes it is the faith of others that works the miracle in us. Theologian Herbert H. Farmer, formerly of Cambridge University, once exclaimed in a lecture, "What are the doubts of Herbert Farmer compared to the faith of Jesus Christ?" The paralytic man's friends had tremendous faith in Christ's power to heal their friend. Jesus gave them high commendation. When we engage in intercessory prayer, we engage not only in unselfish prayer, but in that which may release power as oxygen is released for a hospital patient in an oxygen tent.

The patient described in Mark's Gospel may have suffered from what we now call psychosomatic illness: deep guilt can impair bodily functions. Jesus sensed the hidden cause and forgave his sins.

Here, in this memorable "clinic," someone has said we see: (1) *Faith*—the faith of the sick man's friends. (2) *Fervor*—they were determined to get the sick man to the physician and they raised the roof to do it! (3) *Friendship* is evident here—deep, loyal, healing friendship. They brought their friend to the One who called his followers "friends." What does this say to us in our "lonely crowd" existence today?

## How sensitive can you get?

TEXT: "*His disciples answered, 'You see that the people are crowding you; why do you ask who touched you?'*" (*Mark 5:31, T.E.V.*).

1) "How sensitive can you get?" It could be asked sarcastically, reproachfully. Some of us are hypersensitive. We see blips and hurts on the radar screen of our emotions which are not there! It could be asked by someone intent on measuring our humanity, our Christian maturity. Hal Luccock enjoyed seeing a Poughkeepsie, N.Y., headline describing an automobile accident: "Two persons hurt in route 9-D crash. Peekskill woman suffers consciousness." He was sure it is a great moment when anyone "suffers consciousness," becomes aware of the needs, rights, feelings of others and responds.

2) Of all persons who ever lived, Jesus of Nazareth was the most sensitive to the needs and feelings of others. He saw a crowd as sheep—silly, stubborn, impulsive, sometimes senseless—without a shepherd. The sight and insight moved him "with compassion." When he was in a crowd he always saw the single person in need. So it is in this story which the first three gospels report and which the early church loved. This incident tells us much about Jesus. (See Professor William Barclay's treatment of this section of Mark's Gospel.) What we see in Jesus' concentration on the woman with the chronic disability is, as an unknown Christian said long ago: "God loves each one of us as if there were only one of us to love."

3) How sensitive can *we* get? After all, we cannot carry everybody's burden. Yet this truth must not become an escape hatch from trying to help. It will take it out of us in the racial situation, in dealing with guilt-edged souls, in trying to heal a broken marriage. Our Lord felt what physicians sometimes call a "neural drain"; he knew that power had gone out of him, but it was power to heal. What if through our sensitivity and dedication we can be aides of Christ? He permitted "the tides

of the world's anguish to be forced through the channels of a single heart." As a result, "we touch him in life's throng and press, and we are whole again."

## Stop the treadmill—I want to get off

TEXT: "*The apostles returned and met with Jesus, and told him all they had done and taught. There were so many people coming and going that Jesus and his disciples didn't even have time to eat. So he said to them, 'Let us go off by ourselves to some place where we will be alone and you can rest a while'* " (*Mark 6:30–31*).

Some years ago, a Broadway musical comedy had the title, "Stop the World, I Want to Get Off." Under today's pressures many students as well as many older persons wish they could stop the treadmill of required tasks and extramural engagements and slow down, let up, and recharge physical, emotional, spiritual batteries. Educators express concern that high school students are under such pressures to achieve that their education turns into a rat race. Infants should learn to read, insist some pedagogues. The treadmill may begin earlier than we imagined.

As for college and university students, academic and social pressures seem to increase so that there is little time for wholesome recreation, time to dream great dreams, to engage in creative nonacademic hobbies. One psychiatrist has been quoted as saying: "Educators and parents seem to need to learn all over again that if you worship intellect at the expense of emotional needs, you court disaster." Psychosomatic illnesses and even suicides are increasing, says another, among children and college-age young people who are good or very good students. As for adults, even with a five-day work week plus many weekends in the country or mountains or at the shore, they need to "go by themselves to some place" where they can be alone with the Lord of life and "rest a while."

1) Everyone can master the art of the Religious Society of Friends who "center down" in the greatness, wisdom, love, and renewing power of God. Setting aside even a few minutes in the morning, in the middle of a busy day, and at bedtime to

read a verse or two of a psalm, of the gospels or epistles, of some relevant, devotional contemporary writing, and then quietly to turn all thoughts and feelings toward God, help greatly.

2) However we have changed our Sunday pattern of activity, the corporate worship of God is a priority if we would learn the secret of true renewal. "I come here to find myself," a worshiper says in the words of naturalist John Burroughs, "it is so easy to get lost in the world."

3) We get off the treadmill in order to return with more serenity, insight, stamina, and zeal to engage in "holy worldliness." Jesus Christ gives us rest, not *from* labor, but *in* the midst of it. Retreat to advance, rest for renewal, recreation for re-creation—this is the Christian way.

## Personalism—or what do you see when you look at people?

TEXT: "*. . . Jesus . . . asked him, 'Can you see anything?' The man looked up and said, 'I can see men but they look like trees, walking around'* " (*Mark* 8:23, 24, *T.E.V.*).

1) Crowded urban living tends to dim our sight when it comes to seeing real persons when we look at people. Antidote for this spiritual and moral form of cataracts is what Dr. Paul Tournier, famous Swiss psychiatrist and Christian, calls "the personalism of the Bible." By this the doctor means that when God says to Moses, "I know you by name," God was saying, "I know you as you really are, neither a thing nor an abstraction, nor an idea." Today we tend to look at a man or woman as a prospect, a patient, a case, a fraction of a huge mass. God thinks of us as having a name, an identity, a value.

2) A well-governed state can become too impersonal. We become computer figures. It is essential for the health and joy of people to have the personal touch. In churches the personal touch is indispensable. You can think of examples and ways.

3) Our biblical faith emphasizes that God loves us and sees us as if—as St. Augustine said—there was only one of us to love. Hear the Psalmist: "He determines the number of the stars, he gives to all of them their names" (Psalms 147:4, R.S.V.). But the Psalmist knows that the same God who keeps census

of stars, planets, galaxies, universes also heals the wounds of those deeply hurt: "He heals the brokenhearted, and binds up their wounds" (verse 3). How do we see people? Like the man at stage one of his cure by Jesus—as trees, as things—or as Jesus saw men and women and children—previous persons made in God's own likeness, worth dying for to save?

## What Jesus wanted kept secret

TEXT: "*. . . Jesus did not want anyone to know where he was, because he was teaching his disciples . . .*" (*Mark 9:30, 31, T.E.V.*).

*See also N.E.B.: "Jesus wished it to be kept secret; for he was teaching his disciples, and telling them . . ." (verse 31).*

1) What did Jesus wish to keep secret? The fact of his imminent death and the incredible sequel of the resurrection. It is no longer a secret, but the fact in which millions glory, that although we are sinners Christ died for us.

2) Why did Jesus wish to keep the fact of his sacrificial death secret at that time? It may have been because such a preview of his end would jeopardize God's plan in a world where men had the dangerous gift of freedom. It may be because he knew that his most loyal supporters could not grasp it. Indeed, Mark bluntly reports the disciples' failure to grasp the meaning: "But they did not understand what he said, and were afraid to ask" (verse 32). Is it not still true? In an era of unmatched affluence for many, in the space age with all the tremendous technological advances, many of our contemporaries also do "not understand what he said, and [are] afraid to ask."

3) What is the meaning of the secret? That the human predicament is such that only God's action can untangle it. Evil is everywhere—powerful, subtle, unyielding. Only God, the kind of God who came in Jesus Christ, can overcome evil, "the evil that we do by being us." Mysterious as it is, John Bunyan knew the truth when he said that the Cross is the place where a great burden—the burden of sin—drops from the shoulder of

Christian. The death of Jesus Christ did for all mankind what mankind could not do for itself. So we make our own an unknown poet's lines:

*Upon a life I did not live,*
*Upon a death I did not die,*
*Another's life, another's death,*
*I stake my whole eternity.*

The secret of Christ's cross is now an open secret. It is the sign and disclosure of our human tragedy, our failure, and our sin. It is also the sign and pledge of God's answer, the redemptive answer of God's tremendous love.

## Crisis at the crossroads

TEXT: (*Mark 10:32–34, T.E.V.*). (*See also Luke 9:51.*)

1) Jesus of Nazareth, the one whom Christians call Lord and Savior, had to make choices. He seems closer to us when we recall that he also came to crossroads where decisions had to be made. We must not think that decisions were easy for him. Mark's sketch of Jesus and his first followers outside of Jericho, "on the road, going up to Jerusalem," shows him battling over a crucial choice. Will he go forward now to his nation's chief city where his enemies are concentrated? He was close to what airline pilots used to call "the point of no return." Twice before, Mark reports Jesus predicting his collision with antagonistic authority. He must have known, being the man he was and men being what they are, that if he decided to go to Jerusalem he would be killed. Jesus was not play acting; he need not have died on the cross. He was no "passive pawn of a predestined Providence." See him, then, facing two roads. One leads north to the "fair green hills of Galilee"; the other leads south to Jerusalem—and a cross on which to die. A Scottish preacher of an earlier day, the late James Black, was sure that the real Gethsemane was here, not in the garden. His disciples followed but they were afraid. Was it because of what they saw in that strong, drawn face? He chose: "steadfastly Jesus set his face to go to Jerusalem." He was convinced, as Professor John Knox wrote, that God could use "even his death in bringing

to fulfillment his sovereign purposes." * At the crossroads he accepted the cross.

2) Nations and urban and rural communities face similar choices. Individuals certainly come to crossroads. Jerusalem is not only an ancient city continents away. Figuratively, it is the strategic center to be won in any moral encounter. Chiefly of course, and gloriously, Christ's cross is the symbol of our redemption. In the death of Jesus, God did something we could not do and that we needed to have done; in this divine event power was released to forgive and heal and infuse us with newness of life. No adequate theory exists to explain it. Nevertheless, God's action in Christ on the cross reminds us that it still costs terribly to save any part of the world. The significant goals we reach are the goals toward which we too, with God's help, steadfastly set our faces. What will best advance God's purpose of creating a loving and therefore truly human family on this planet? Will it be taking the road to Galilee, or to Jerusalem?

3) Churches face the crossroads. Even when "the secular bit" is hammered from many sides and we know that our urban culture demands something more than the traditional "establishment," which road shall we as a congregation of Christ's church take? We are not asked to submit to crucifixion in obedience to God's will, but we are asked to face sharp issues, strong opposition to Christlike justice and love, and to pay often a high price for our loyalty to our Lord. To deny ourselves means not to hate ourselves but to stop taking and to start giving.

4) Evangelists may leave us cold when they announce loud and clear that this is the hour of decision. But it is. Indecisiveness is sickening and for most of us unnecessary. Recall the young girl taking a personality test. To the question "Are you indecisive?" she answered, after chewing her pencil, "Yes and no." But to the crucial questions it must be Yes or No. Professor Gordon Allport of Harvard quotes a counselor as saying that after years of experience he realized that the most revealing single questions he ever asked a client was, "Where do you want to be five years from now?" Where *do* you want to be? To what goal are you headed? Do you know where you

* *The Death of Christ* (Nashville: Abingdon Press, 1958).

want to be going and have you chosen the One who will be going with you if you choose Jerusalem?

## Challenge to the power structure

TEXT: (*Mark 10:32–45, T.E.V.*).

1) It is an unforgettable picture etched in contrasting colors. Jesus, their Master, striding ahead purposefully to challenge the authorities located in the nation's capital; his disciples hanging back, timid, hesitant, bewildered. Jesus had set his course and was moving irrevocably toward journey's end. Little wonder that at least two of his followers misunderstood the nature of the kingdom. Had they not been so wrong in their understanding they would not have asked for places in the hierarchy they imagined would be established. Any hierarchy would be in God's hands and based not on privilege but on service.

2) We see here a challenge to the powers of that society. The challenge is still being made. Only those who are servants will know the enduring satisfactions of God's society. As William Neil, biblical scholar, puts it, "Jesus puts himself in the forefront as the type and pattern, the Son of Man who makes himself a servant, that all the sons of men may become sons of God."

A fivefold division for treatment of this passage has been suggested by Arthur E. Dalton: (1) The Journey onwards. (2) The Jesus before them. (3) The Joy denied them. (4) The Judgment awaiting him. (5) The Justification promised them.* Professor William Barclay sees in this same passage a vivid portrait of Jesus. We see (1) the loneliness of Jesus; (2) the courage of Jesus; (3) "the personal magnetism of Jesus."

## It's the greatest

TEXT: "*. . . If one of you wants to be great, he must be the servant of the rest; and if one of you wants to be first, he must be the slave of all.*" (*Mark 10:43–44, T.E.V.*). (*See also verse 45.*)

* *Brief and to the Point* by A. E. Dalton (Grand Rapids: Kregel Publications, 1962).

## [48] It's the greatest

Two friends were discussing churches. One was asked what kind of a church was the one he attended. Enthusiastically (believe it or not!), he responded: "It's the greatest!"

If this evaluation of a church was made to you, and you pressed the appraiser to define what he meant, what is your guess as to what makes a local church truly great? The Head and Founder of the church which bears his name gives us the answer in true although general terms. When he described true greatness in a person Jesus contrasted the "power structure"—"the men who are considered rulers of the people [who] have power over them"—with the genuinely great. "If one of you wants to be great, he must be the servant of the rest." In God's kingdom the question is not "How many people can we control?" but "How much service can I give?" Even a congregation of Christian people sometimes forgets that it is to be a servant people. Some years ago a men's movement in Canada chose the name A.O.T.S., initial letters of the phrase, "as one that serves." This is a good definition of a Christian.

What are the elements in a great church, however small it may be in membership and income? A servant people may well be marked by (1) vital, worthy worship. The public worship of God is the priority; all else is derivative. This is the reason for a church's existence: to offer God the most acceptable prayer and praise of which it is capable.

Such worship includes (2) Christian, biblically-based proclamation of the Good News of God in Jesus Christ. Joined with preaching that is Christian—and therefore relevant—would be (unless we make the Religious Society of Friends an exception) a vital sacramental life. By this phrase is meant the faithful administration of the two sacraments most of us believe to be authorized by scripture. Sacramental life is nourished in regular and frequent partaking of Holy Communion (or the Lord's Supper or the Eucharist), but it expresses itself in regarding all of life as sacramental.

True greatness in a church consists also in (3) its involvement in the world, here and now. Solitary religion is not Christianity, nor is isolation from the 'dirty business" of politics, economics, social concerns. To be Christian is to care, and caring means involvement in the human situation on "both sides of the track."

A great church is a church in which (4) all walls erected by culture, money, status, and sectarianism are transcended in a living, loving, inclusive fellowship. Such a community practices acceptance of those some might consider unacceptable. Such a *koinonia* welcomes those who are unwelcome in some of the "best" circles. The Christian church believes in and demonstrates the communion of saints, and the saints include Christians who may be difficult and all too human, as well as those "going on to perfection" in the church triumphant.

One of the nineteenth-century "heretics," Father George Tyrell, said that at the end of our day, God will not ask us, "What kind of church did you belong to?" but rather, "What kind of church did you long for?" Well?

## On the alert

TEXT: *"What I say to you then, I say to all: Watch!" (Mark 13:37, T.E.V.).*

What are you looking for during the weeks before Christmas? Perhaps an unexpected gift, a bonus from the company. You might settle for less extravagance on your part and on the part of other family members! The season of Advent historically struck the note of being on the alert for the final coming of Christ at the end of the age. To most of us and to a majority of church members this is not a lively concern. The future is in God's hands. If and when history ends, we may hope that all will be well with us. Nevertheless, even a brief examination of Christ's recorded sayings points to his conviction that there would be an end—the end—soon or late. Was it because the Lord did not want us to settle down and assume that everything would be "business as usual" forever? Certainly, like the commander of troops who knows that the enemy is powerful, subtle, near, Jesus repeatedly urged his first followers to watch. Paul takes up the same emphasis: "Be alert, stand firm in the faith, be brave, be strong" (1 Corinthians 16:13).

What are we to look for? The late John Baillie wrote that there are three things for which our Lord desired us to be particularly on the alert. (1) The first is opportunity, and that comes to those who are waiting for it. This is the opportunity, not for wealth, prestige, promotion, but for service. Ask what you can do for your country certainly; but also for your church, for the great worldwide cause of Christ, for the community where we live, for persons who need help. (2) Christ wants us to be on the alert for temptation. "Keep watch, and pray, so that you will not fall into temptation" (Matthew 26:41). The devil, or if you prefer, the devilish forces in life are skillful at ambushing Christ's followers. Surprise attacks just when we feel safest are the devil's specialty. Our secret weapon is prayer. (3) Christ desires us to be on the alert for truth. It is to the man or woman, the boy or girl, who is open and searching for truth that truth is revealed.* "Ask, and you will receive; seek, and you will find; knock, and the door will be opened to you" (Matthew 7:7).

Much doubt and much uncertainty today may be due to our refusal to keep alert. Long ago, as an undergraduate, I remember Miss Margaret Slattery giving immense help by saying, "Truth reveals itself to a mind that approaches mystery without prejudice." But we must approach, and we must be on the alert —open, sensitive, responsive. Emile Cammaerts, who moved, as did C. S. Lewis, from atheism to Christian faith, said, "There is a healthy element in the tradition of the Church which warns Christians to beware both of the poetical metaphor and concrete materialization. If human remembrance does not go far enough, human spiritualism goes a great deal too far. There may be hidden forces behind the veil of nature, but, whether good or evil, their true essence remains a mystery. God alone knows, and it is safer to leave miracles to him."† Advent says Christ is near. Christmas declares Christ is here. Be alert!

## "What are we to do with the boy that will be born?"

TEXT: (*Luke 1:26–33, T.E.V.; Judges 13:8, R.S.V.*).

To famed Scottish preacher and professor emeritus James S. Stewart we owe choice of this text. It is the prayer of Manoah when he learned from a divine messenger that he and his wife were to expect a child who would be one of their people's great leaders and deliverers. The child was Samson. Cen-

* *Christian Devotion* by John Baillie (New York: Charles Scribner's Sons, 1962), pp. 52–60.

† *Upon This Rock*, by Emile Cammaerts (New York: Harper & Row, Publishers, 1943), p. 69.

turies later God sent another and a greater deliverer. He, too, would come as a child. Every nation's character and destiny would be disclosed by the way they received this Child Jesus. As the old priest Simeon predicted, "This child is chosen by God for the destruction and the salvation of many in Israel; he will be a sign from God which many will speak against . . ." (Luke 2:34).

In Advent Christ comes again. Momentous is the challenge of his coming. To the question "What shall we do with the child that shall be born?" at least three different answers continue to be made.

1) There is Herod's answer. It is the response of hostility. "Let him be destroyed!" Today, those enamored of paganism, of the way of ruthlessness, of violence, want this Christ out of the way. Milder opponents of Christ and his ethic and gospel resemble the dauphin in George Bernard Shaw's *St. Joan;** they wish he would shut up and go home. As the church engages in mission within the world it meets with resistance and fierce opposition. As Professor Stewart remarks, Herod should have faced another question: "What will this child grown to manhood do to me and my cause and kingdom?"

2) The innkeeper's answer was the answer many make today. It is the response of apathy, of indifference. "What shall we do to and with this child?" We are simply too busy to do anything. To how many in our age and in our community is Christ and his way not a danger but an irrelevance?

3) The answer Simeon made is the answer God wants us to make, as individuals, as a community of Christians. "In the temple, Simeon took the child in his arms, gave thanks to God: '. . . Lord . . . with my own eyes I have seen your salvation, / Which you have made ready in the presence of all peoples: . . .'" (Luke 2:28–31).

Will you make the answer of commitment?†

## "You'd better come home"

TEXT: "*When the angels went away from them back into heaven, the shepherds said to one another, 'Let us go to*

* (New York: Brentano's, 1924).

† Adapted from James S. Stewart, "The Challenge of His Coming," in *The Wind of the Spirit* (London: Hodder & Stoughton, Ltd., 1968), pp. 170–79.

*Bethlehem and see this thing that has happened, that the Lord has told us.' So they hurried off and found Mary and Joseph, and saw the baby lying in the manger"* (*Luke 2:15, 16, T.E.V.*).

1) Mobility as well as anonymity may be salient features of our culture and society. Harvey Cox and others have so assured us, and the furniture movers' business confirms it. Nevertheless, we respond to the words which English "pop singer" Petulah Clark belted out on air waves in a recent year: "You'd better come home." Her counsel was directed to a lover who had had his fun in other places. It is when we have found much of the so-called "fun" of being on our own, and perhaps in some far country, that we know we had better come home. But what or who is home? And how do we get there?

2) Christmas, or more accurately the Christ Event which we celebrate at Christmas, is God's way of saying, "For your own sake and for the world's and for mine, you'd better come home." You mean, we say, to our best self? to a "transvaluation of values"? to a more balanced life? And God seems to say, Yes, all that, but now come home to reality. Recall Isaac Watts' familiar use of Psalm 90 in the hymn, "O God, our help in ages past." In it he speaks of God not only as "shelter from the stormy blast" but "our eternal home." This is why, like the shepherds, we take our way in imaginative faith to a stable in what is now a Jordan village. On the first Christmas it was so simple, so rustic, and everyone so unsophisticated. Gilbert K. Chesterton had a story, *Manalive,* in which the hero deliberately traveled around the world in order to discover his own house and garden. Whether a member of a jet set or not, we usually find the wonderful, essential things at home. When we need to connect with reality, the creative, redemptive Reality we call God, it is also true. To quote Chesterton's best-loved poem, "Home at Last": "To the place where God was homeless, / And all men are at home."*

3) If we can possibly manage it, we come home at Christmas. Think of the boys and men in Asia, in Europe, in Africa, whose homes are over here and who would give almost anything to be home for Christmas. But our true home is in God. Wise Men and shepherds in the Nativity stories found that a star-led journey ended at a manger and a baby. This is more

* "The House of Christmas" in *Collected Poems* by G. K. Chesterton (New York: Dodd, Mead & Co., 1932).

than a pretty legend. This is revelation of God's wisdom that we find God, that we are at home—accepted, welcomed, loved—not in distant stars, not "up there," but in simple, loving giving of the unsurpassed gift. When we respond with the gift of our own lives to God-in-a-human life and to the cause he embodied and taught, we are in our true home.

## Return, don't just go back!

TEXT: "*The shepherds went back, singing praises to God for all they had heard and seen; it had been just as the angel had told them*" (*Luke* 2:20, T.E.V.).

On the Sunday after Christmas, the Word of the Lord comes to us in colloquial phrase: "Don't just go back to the everyday world, but return—with the meaning and joy, the promise and commission of the Christ in Christmas." Of course, the angels had to go away—there must have been heavenly missions to undertake. Of course, the shepherds had to go back to their work. The Wise Men, too, could not remain forever in adoring worship of the child born to be king. And Mary and Simeon had to return to their duties.

Professor R. E. O. White of the Baptist Theological College of Scotland has a fourfold division of this theme you may care to make your own and fill with content. (1) "The shepherds went back, singing praises to God . . ." (2) The Wise Men returned, another way. Did we come as seekers, as they did, and do we return as those who have found? (3) Mary returned—pondering these things in her heart. Will we go on exploring, or be content with a Christmas gospel only? (4) Simeon returned, and was ready for the next great dimension of life, vindicated and content.

## It could happen in church!

TEXT: (*Luke* 2:22–38, *T.E.V.*).

1) Let's face it: many persons are sure that nothing creative, revoluntionary, world-changing could ever happen in church. In it they see stuffy, smug people engaging in a kind of mutual massage of ruffled emotions. Worship in "conventional churches" (say the critics) is an escape hatch for timid souls

unable to cope with the world in its abrasive reality. The preacher or priest is a mild-mannered man concerned with making a docile people ever more docile. If he becomes prophetic he runs the risk of harassment and eventual loss of employment.

Look now at Luke's account of the Jewish purification ceremony. Something tremendous happened in and to the two persons on the temple staff. And it happened in church, in the temple. Harsh things were said by Christ in his adult career concerning orthodox religion, the temple and Jerusalem, but never did he forsake the "establishment." It was in what we call church that Simeon and Anna recognized the Christ in Mary's arms.

2) Simeon is described as upright, devout, expectant, and spiritually endowed (verse 25). From the *nunc dimittis* (verses 29–32) we learn what this discerning man saw in Jesus. Christ was—and is—deliverance, light, and glory. Writes D. W. Cleverley-Ford, "This is the gospel; the gospel to be preached and the gospel to be interpreted. But deliverance, the illumination and the glory will not be achieved without suffering."*

3) Anna recognized God uniquely in the human life of Jesus through her own personal devotion within the church. She was so convinced and thrilled by her discovery that "she talked about the child to all who were looking for the liberation of Jerusalem." Don't write off the church as a place where revelation is made and lives are changed. But why were there only two persons in church who made the tremendous discovery of Christ?

## Packaged souls in a packaged society

TEXT: "*. . . This child is chosen by God for the destruction and the salvation of Israel; he will be a sign from God which many people will speak against, and so reveal their secret thoughts. And sorrow, like a sharp sword, will break your own heart*" (*Luke* 2:34, 35).

In an interesting and provocative essay, Russel Lynes deals with what he calls "The Packaged Society." "Everything in America, including people, comes packaged," contends Mr. Lynes, "and the package, by and large, is designed to conceal

* A *Reading in Saint Luke's Gospel* (Philadelphia: J. B. Lippincott Company, 1967), p. 50.

and not to reveal its contents or at least to make the contents look a great deal better than they are."* Almost everything comes packaged, including ideas, services, pleasures, places, vices. Indeed, it may be that "we are all items in a national supermarket—categorized, processed, labeled, priced, and readied for merchandising." Even universities and colleges offer a sort of academic "big economy package!" Personal packaging is an ancient art, and most of us like to wrap ourselves in some kind of wrapping which will create a certain "image." Friends and foes alike package ideas which they hope many will buy. One observer suggests that we may not go for certain packaged ideas in our political shops, not because of the contents, but because the packaging is distasteful. Consider these words of Mr. Lynes: "One wonders if there has ever been a total society that has taken such precautions against revealing what it can conveniently conceal."

1) The Advent season reminds us of One who came that he might reveal the secret of reality. Reverently we may say that Jesus Christ was the human container of the great God, creator, redeemer, life of mankind. God wrapped up his love and wisdom, his justice and design in the personality of one born to a Jewish maid at the first Christmas.

2) As devout Simeon said when he saw the child Jesus, "he will expose the secrets of many hearts." Somehow the Light of the world searches our inner selves, introduces us to ourselves.

3) Encounter with Jesus Christ also convinces us that the many truths which some wish to conceal from the "rank and file" of mankind, God unwraps and shows plainly. True, mystery remains. Our thoughts are far from God's thoughts. Nevertheless, when we approach mystery without prejudice, looking at the mysterious and the perplexing with something of the eyes of Christ, insight comes. When the first disciples returned from their mission Jesus was thrilled. Says Luke: "At that moment Jesus himself was inspired with joy, and exclaimed: 'O Father, Lord of Heaven and earth, I thank you for hiding these things from the clever and intelligent and for showing them to mere children!' . . ." (Luke 10:20 J. B. P.).

4) In the early church as in the medieval church, the Advent season had somber notes of judgment pealing. Today, for most of us, such emphasis seems unnecessary and even

* *Harper's Magazine*, August, 1966.

sub-Christian. Yet is it not reassuring to believe with the scriptures that when all the wrappings are removed in another dimention of life eternal, and we shall know as we shall be known, the God we have come to know in Jesus Christ will judge the secrets of our hearts? Writes the Apostle Paul to the Christians in Rome: ". . . in the day . . . when God will judge men's secret lives by Jesus Christ . . ." (Romans, 2:16, J. B. P.). We may act responsibly and seek always God's justice, confident that he who is our Judge is also our Redeemer.

## Get this habit for your health's sake

TEXT: "*Then Jesus went to Nazareth, where he had been brought up, and on the Sabbath day he went as usual to the synagogue*" (*Luke 4:16, T.E.V.*).

What does the word "habit" bring to mind? To many who are aware of the use of LSD, marijuana, barbiturates, and other drugs, it suggests something bad, something unhealthy—an addiction to slow poison. Apart from this clinical connotation, "habit" connotes a rut. We are, we say, as our fathers said before us, "creatures of habit." So much of life is dull because it is habitual. True, a case for the defense of habit can be made. To be habitually honest, thoughtful, responsible, kind, is to be a good character, a citizen who helps hold the fabric of decent society together. Concerning evil habits, the colloquialism applies: "Kick the habit!" But Luke records an interesting fact concerning Jesus of Nazareth. When he came to his home town, he "went to synagogue on the Sabbath day as he regularly did" (N.E.B.).

1) Get this habit for your health's sake. Health implies wholeness. No human being is whole or complete, wholesome or healthy, who suffers from imbalance. Imbalance is another way of indicating deficiency. What men live by—according to Dr. Richard C. Cabot, sometime professor at Harvard Medical School—are the four essentials labeled Love, Work, Play, Worship. We are animals, but much more. We must have something, someone to adore, to worship, to love and serve, greater than any human or material object. Said a great Russian of the past century, "Without God a man cannot bear the burden of himself." Take time to be whole, by making habitual your attendance at church and participation in its worship of God.

2) Get this habit without ignoring, or rebelling at, much you may find in the visible church which disturbs, irritates, or even repels you. Jesus must have found many things in his synagogue and in all other synagogues of his time which grated on him. Much in the ecclesiastical leadership would cause him to disagree; yet Jesus went to the synagogue as was his habit. Wrote a New Testament commentator on this verse: "The worship of the synagogue might be far from perfect; yet Jesus never omitted to join himself to God's worshiping people on God's day." If he found this habit so important, our frequently spasmodic attendance may need review.

3) Get the habit of regular, frequent worship with God's people that this habit may be a reinforcement of the best kind of action Monday through Saturday. The Rev. W. D. Cattanach of St. George's West Church of Scotland gives me this pertinent word from a nineteenth-century writer, "The most intellectual of men are moved quite as much by the circumstances they are used to as by their own will. . . . We could not do every day out of our own heads all we have to do. We should accomplish nothing, for all our energies would be frittered away in minor attempts at petty improvement."* In this time when churchgoing is considered something "for the birds"—pious, otherworldly, insecure "birds"—it is salutary to remember that our Lord needed the support of such a habit, as he did of private prayer. This is no advocacy of routine religion. It is a serious plea to emulate Christ who went to his church on the appointed day as his custom was. Churchgoing may not be equated with Christian living, but there is a direct relationship between the two. Get this habit and prove for yourself that it is easier to keep on the beam of Christian ethical living, of deep interior communion with the Spirit, of commitment to Christ in today's world, when you are habitual in your worship and prayer.

## If you say so

TEXT: " '*Master, Simon answered, we worked hard all night long and caught nothing. But if you say so, I will let down the nets*' " (*Luke* 5:5, T.E.V.).

Wouldn't you like to know how Simon looked when he made that response to Jesus? Was his an expression of high

* Walter Bagehot, *The English Constitution* (London: Oxford University Press, 1933).

expectancy, of complete confidence? Or did the big fisherman wear a look of resignation or of unhappy compliance? After all, Simon and his colleagues were experienced fishermen and Jesus was a carpenter by trade, a landsman by lifelong habit. In any case Simon recognized the word of an authority. Jesus spoke as no other man he had ever heard. He was right about so much that Simon was sure that if Jesus gave even a wild suggestion it must be followed. ". . . if you say so . . ."

What about those of us who "profess and call ourselves Christian"? Again and again Christ has proved right. We trusted him when he told us to change our minds, to change our way of thinking and living and follow him. The results justified the venture, didn't they? When he tells us to "push the boat out further to the deep water" for a catch, are we willing to be fools for his sake? Think of some of his directives which to the sophisticated pagan seem so absurd: "Love your enemies"; "Resist not evil"; ". . . give first place to his Kingdom and to what he requires, and he will provide you with all these other things" (Matthew 6:33). " 'Do not be worried and upset,' Jesus told them. 'Believe in God, and believe also in me' " (John 14:1).

Ralph W. Sockman tells about a lawyer friend of his who, when he was a small boy, was brought by his father to New York City. To keep from getting lost in the busy, crowded streets the little fellow held to his father's finger. After a time he grew tired, and his steps began to slow down. He looked up at his father and said, "Father, you'll have to take hold of my hand now for I can't hold on much longer." God in Christ holds us when we cannot hold on ourselves. It may seem elementary, but if we cannot hold on we cannot continue fishing for him or engaging in any other enterprise. We begin by saying, ". . . if you say so, I will . . ."

## The high cost of Christlike loving

TEXT: (*Luke 9:51–62, T.E.V.*).

Jesus was scrupulously honest about the cost of membership in God's kingdom. A public relations man might well urge him to soften the demands, reduce the price, emphasize the rewards. But Christ never hid his scars to win a follower or conceal the harsh facts of life with him and for him. To three men who seemed to be "live prospects" for his cause and company Jesus "told it as it is."

1) To the man who vowed he would support Jesus wherever it led, Jesus said, "Count the cost." Do we pitch the demands of membership in Christ's church anything like as high? Do we offer the spiritual equivalents of trading stamps, bonus payments here or hereafter, and peace of mind? If we told the truth completely we would certainly have fewer members, but they would be better members, more committed Christians in this revolutionary world.

2) To man number two Jesus seemed to speak abrasively. When Jesus told him to follow, he said, "I surely will after my father has died." His father may not have been sick! Jesus underlined the truth that there is a moment of decision. That crucial moment may not recur. "Action now!" is the signal we receive from Christ.

3) To the third "prospect" he said, "Don't look back!" Face the sunrise with Christ. You are either *on* the way with the Son of Man or you are *in* the way.

It is costly to follow Christ. Recall Dietrich Bonhoeffer's book, *The Cost of Discipleship.** The symbol of the Christian life is not a couch but a cross; and a cross was not jewelry when Christ spoke of it, accepted it, died on it. Never can we use the slogan, "Back to Christ!" Instead, "Forward to Christ! Forward with Christ!" To march with him into the kind of society he desires, and man must have for his survival and newness of life, takes all there is of us. As the great hymn "When I Survey the Wondrous Cross" affirms, this man Christ Jesus "demands my life, my soul, my all."

## New every morning

TEXT: *"Give us day by day the food we need"* (*Luke 11:3, T.E.V.*).

Famed musician Pablo Casals was visited one day by a man who was astonished to see the veteran cellist playing scales over and over. He expressed surprise that one so skilled, experienced, and gifted should engage in such a dull routine of practicing. Said the master: "My son, in playing the cello the problem is to get from one note to the next. This is why I practice scales every day."

* (New York: The Macmillan Company, 1948), p. 31.

1) This is our problem: to get from one note to the next, from one challenge to the next, from one day to the next. Jesus our Lord taught us to live by the wise rule of one day at a time. He taught his disciples, "Give us day by day the food we need" (Luke 11:3). "So do not worry about tomorrow," he directed, "it will have enough worries of its own. There is no need to add to the troubles each day brings" (Matthew 6:34). In a famous address to medical students the late Sir William Osler (Canada's gift to the United States and to England, one of the "big four" of Johns Hopkins University's medical school) urged that we learn to "live with daytight compartments" as on an ocean liner.

2) One of the tremendous facts of spiritual experience is that God provides all the resources we need every morning. Read the hauntingly beautiful verses in the third chapter of the Old Testament book with the sad name "Lamentations." "Great is thy faithfulness!" exclaimed the writer as he reflected on this fact. We can live one day at a time because we know that as our day so shall our strength be. This is why over a century ago John Keble wrote the hymn, "New every morning is the love our waking and uprising prove."

3) One aspect of this truth is underlined by the ancient story of the manna provided for the Israelites (Exodus 16). Whatever the manna may have been, it was the equivalent of bread. Meat at night (quails that covered the ground) and manna in the morning helped Moses the food controller meet the food-shortage crisis. In the absence of refrigeration Moses instructed the people to gather only sufficient manna for each day. Can we do more? Is it possible to store up resources of the spirit in advance? Do we not need to rely on daily prayer, interior discipline, the food for mind and soul God provides each returning day? A young pastor asked an extremely busy older minister how he managed to stay on top of every day's problems, harassments, and worries. The mature Christian answered quietly, "The manna falls."

## Do you know these pictures of the Crucifixion?

TEXT: "*I have a baptism to receive, and how distressed I am until it is over!*" (*Luke* 12:50, *T.E.V.*).

## Do you know these pictures of the Crucifixion? [61]

The late president of Union Theological Seminary, New York, Dr. Henry Sloane Coffin, told of a newspaper editor who went to see the Passion Play at Oberammergau. He came away from it saying to himself: "This is the story which has transformed the world." He seemed to hear an echo from the Bavarian mountains: "Yes, and will transform it." Why is it so? There have been many other deaths of noble men and women, many martyrdoms, many innocent persons done to death by evil men. History has a long roll of those who died rather than betray the truth or the cause of humanity to which they were utterly committed. We may have clues to the answer in the pictures of his death which Jesus himself drew.

New Testament scholar Professor Archibald M. Hunter points out that our Lord saw his suffering and death in three ways. (1) Jesus pictured his death on Calvary as a *baptism:* "I have a baptism to receive, and how distressed I am until it is over!" (Luke 12:50). He asks his disciples if they are able to be baptized with his baptism (Mark 10:38). Here, plainly, "baptism" is a figure of speech denoting death. Luke reports Jesus' saying that only so can the fire of the gospel be kindled.

2) Jesus gives us the second picture of his death as he sees it. He sees it as a *cup* that God has given him to drink. "Can you drink the cup that I must drink?" he asks his disciples (Mark 10:38). In Gethsemane's garden, Jesus cries in agony, "Father! . . . my Father! All things are possible for you. Take this cup away from me. But not what I want, what you want" (Mark 14:36). In the Old Testament, seventeen out of twenty metaphorical uses of the word "cup" denote divinely-appointed suffering, even punishment (see Isaiah 51:17, 22). Dr. Hunter feels that Jesus used the picture of the cup as the cup of God's opposition, even wrath, against human sin. Somehow the Father had to put into Jesus' hands the cup our sins had made. "He tasted in all its naked horror the wrath of God against the sin of man." *

3) The third picture of his death depicted by Jesus is a *road* to be traveled. "The Son of Man will die as the Scriptures say he will . . ." (Mark 14:21). What road in scripture does he mean? It is the way of the cross, the path of humiliation and death. Was this not mapped out five centuries before in Isaiah's portait of the Suffering Servant of God?

* *The Work and Words of Jesus* (Philadelphia: The Westminster Press, 1951), p. 97.

All of these pictures make clear that Jesus believed his death to be a necessity. True, there are two other significant sayings, perhaps the most important: that concerning the ransom (Mark 10:45) and the saying about the covenant, spoken over the cup at the Last Supper (Mark 14:24). See also Paul's quotation of that which he said he "received" from the Lord (1 Corinthians 11:25). If we see these pictures we may be able to see with the eyes of spiritual insight and faith that because of Christ's death we and all God's children are able to enter into the new order of relations between God and men and to know the tremendous benefit of sins forgiven and renewed friendship with God.

## For mercy's sake!

TEXT: (*Luke 13:10–21, T.E.V.*). *For sermon use verses 10 through 17.*

1) The woman was helpless in her disability.

2) Her misery called forth the Lord's mercy. Have you seen Christ today? You have if you have seen someone helped or healed by one of his aides, even when the person so used is unaware of being used by the divine Spirit. To Jesus, as to every sensible follower, it matters not what day of the week it is if the action is indicated. But the leader of the religious community was hopeless in his obstructive stand. He sounds like the theatrical caricature of a present-day rector's warden, clerk of session, or chairman of some official board! Couldn't we have the healing done on one of the six weekdays available? Why engage in such secular action on the holy day!

3) The petty, hypocritical spirit of the synagogue president was blasted by our Lord. We need to have the littleness and hypocrisy in our own lives exposed by the Son of God. We, too, cavil and carp because we are not yet as compassionate as we would like others to think.

4) Christ's action and his unmasking of the self-righteous made the people happy. "His answer made all his enemies ashamed of themselves, while all the people rejoiced over every wonderful thing he did" (Luke 13:17).

## When we feel lost at home

TEXT: "*. . . the younger son sold his part of the property and left home with the money. He went to a country far away, where he wasted his money in reckless living. He spent everything he had. Then a severe famine spread over that country, and he was left without a thing*" (*Luke 15:13, 14, T.E.V.*).

In our time many sensitive, intelligent young people have what is sometimes called an "identity crisis." They wonder who they really are; what goals they should choose. Indeed, these contemporary prodigal sons and daughters are not so much "prodigal" or wayward, as bewildered, disenchanted, "lost" even when at home or on a college campus.

Why do some of us feel "lost"—in the sense of not having found what it's all about?

1) Change and dismay all around is all that many of us can see. No wonder: since 1945 more technological advances and changes have occurred than in all previous eras of human history. Nor are the changes only technological. What of the changing family, the so-called "new morality," the updating of vast ecclesiastical structures once considered immovable and unchangeable? Consider the population explosion, the rise of new nations and of a new nationalism, the greater life-expectancy in the western world, the greater number of "over sixty-five's" and teen-agers, the racial revolution, continuing wars. Many feel they don't have a point of view and know not where they're going because of the loss of vital Christian faith.

2) Like the prodigal son in a far country, disenchantment with living aimlessly hits us. As the eminent European psychiatrist Viktor Frankl makes clear, a basic drive in human beings sends us on a search for meaning. Life, or more accurately God, says to us, "You don't know what you're missing." At least a world of significant meaning awaits us. The supreme authority on life, Jesus Christ, was sure that if we seriously and persistently asked, sought, knocked on the door of the Interpreter's House, we would find meaning. Sincerity in our quest, openness of mind and spirit, willingness to change our mind and way of thinking and living, and we would find ourselves going somewhere.

3) This is why Christ is essential to all who would be

going somewhere significant in their working faith, their daily work and leisure, their human relationships, their eternal destiny.

The late James Moffatt translated the words of the Apostle Paul (rendered in the King James Version, "For to me to live is Christ"): "Christ means life to me." With Christ and—as Paul would say—"in Christ," making him our guide, our teacher, our Savior and Lord. We realize that life is no blot or blank for us, that it means intensely and that it means good; that to give ourselves away in Christlike love is really living; that to be obedient servants of One who is uniquely the Suffering Servant of God, in terms of today's world. Also, we are impelled to maintain the two-way communication with him which is prayer and worship—this is to go somewhere.

Yes, as the famous old catechism put it, our reason for existence is "to glorify God and enjoy him forever." We do this through and in Christ. He that does his will will know what life is all about.

## You can go home again

TEXT: "*I will get up and go to my father . . .*" (*Luke 15:18, T.E.V.*). "*And the ransomed of the Lord shall return . . .*" (*Isaiah 35:10, R.S.V.*).

1) In a profound sense, once we are adults we cannot go home again to the home we knew in childhood and youth. In this respect, Thomas Wolfe was right in the title of his famous novel, *You Can't Go Home Again*. In our present time of troubles, many are afflicted with despair or nostalgia. The nostalgic sign with the poet, "Backward, turn backward, O Time, in your flight, Make me a child again, just for the night!" But regression to the infantile is no cure for spiritual sickness. Indeed, if we could return to the home of our childhood we would be disillusioned, discontented, dismayed. Even if the home remained unchanged, we would be different in so many ways.

2) Yet, in a profound spiritual sense, we can go home again. There is a homing instinct in birds and animals. They seem to have a kind of built-in radar which guides them in their journeys. Robert Ardrey* writes that when a bird known as the

* *The Territorial Imperative* (New York: Atheneum Publishers, 1966).

Manx shearwater from Skokholm Island off the coast of Wales was transported by a Cambridge scientist by airliner to Harvard University, the shearbird was back in his burrow on Skokholm Island twelve and one-half days later! The bird had traveled 3,050 miles at an average speed of 244 miles per day. Do you recall reading about the albatross community on Midway Island which caused so much trouble to our naval jet aircraft? Wildlife experts tried to attach the albatross' loyalty to Japan, the Philippines, the Marianas Islands, and Hawaii, but within a month the birds were back home after flights of 3,000 miles! Of course, human beings have no such interior programming in regard to physical locations. Have we a need for roots which we have tended to ignore or minimize? What if, in spite of loud denials to the contrary, the living God is, as the hymn "O God, our help in ages past" affirms, following the writer of Psalm 90, "our eternal home"? Is it accidental that the Bible's most famous story is the one told by Jesus about a prodigal who found his way home?

3) This is the primary mission of Christ's church in all its branches and expressions: to help guide the misplaced and the homeless to their true home. A word sometimes given to this mission and commission is evangelism. It is a word always in need of definition and interpretation. Evangelism is much more than singing about "Coming home." It involves such "secular" action as better housing, finding jobs and job training for those now lost and wandering, healing sick persons, and much more. It also involves assuring men and women of all degrees of culture and position that Jesus Christ came that we might go home to our true home.

One of Scotland's contemporary Christian leaders is the Reverend W. D. Cattanach. He told recently of a girl offender sixteen years old and already possessed of a criminal record. She was "radically insecure . . . with no religious upbringing at all. She had no roots or identity at all because she was an illegitimate child. She did not know who she was, she had no name." After instruction, she requested and received Christian baptism. Thereafter the difference was marked. She told Mr. Cattanach, her counselor, that it was all right now because she had "come home." She belonged now. In her spiritual adviser's words, "she had touched the springs of our existence and she knew it."

[66]

## How far can you see?

TEXT: "*So he got up and started back to his father. He was still a long way from home when his father saw him; his heart was filled with pity and he ran, threw his arms around his son, and kissed him*" (*Luke* 15:20, T.E.V.).

1) Longsightedness as far as our physical vision is concerned may not always be an advantage. When it comes to seeing persons in their need it is the mark of a Christian. "Bless me and my wife, my son John and his wife; we four and no more" is not the prayer of a man "in Christ." To "see" in imagination based on facts those in desperate plight in Southeast Asia, in Africa, in the ghettos of North American cities, in the communities where we live—this requires something like treatment by a divine ophthalmologist. It is easy and more comfortable to see only those closest to us. It is tragic when we do not see someone we know who seems to us to be "way out" now "on the beam," or, as Jesus said in his greatest story of "the waiting father," on the way home to reality, to newness of life. This is what moves us about the prodigal's father in the parable. "So he got up and started back to his father." Few of his erstwhile cronies would dream that this was his destination. But his father knew. "He was still a long way from home when his father saw him . . ." We are quick to see when someone, or an entire group, is in a far country of rebellion, riotous living, degradation. How far can we see when such persons right-about-face, start on the road to profound change and renewal?

2) All of us are "a long way from" God's goal for us. Who isn't in a "far country" of selfishness, of indifference to wrong in our own relationships, in society around us? The biblical analysis is realistic. "All have sinned." But the Bible, like the great God it makes known, has a tremendous optimism rooted in a true pessimism when it comes to human nature and the human situation. Wherever we are, however far we are from Christ and his ethic and faith, we need not remain "far off." We too can change our minds, or, more accurately, open our minds to the life-changing power of God's Spirit. We too can say, "I will get up and go to my father" (Luke 15:18). Then we realize the long-distance love of the divine Father.

3) While we are still a long way off, making this detour, stopping too long en route, the Father sees us and his great

heart of love goes out to us. This is not dreamed up by a pious sentimentalist or some hot revivalist; this is the way God is. He waits and watches and hopes and believes that we will come to ourselves, our true selves, and then to him, and to the family from which we have been estranged. (Sermon builders who have not done so should read books on this theme by Helmut Thielicke* and by J. Wallace Hamilton.†)

## Handling guilt-edged living

TEXT: "*'Father,' the son said, 'I have sinned against God and against you'* . . ." (*Luke* 15:21, T.E.V.).

1) Not long ago an American woman wrote some verses in which she expressed the wish that there might be someone available who could hear confession. What she wanted was someone who would unite the best qualities of a God, a mother, a priest, a friend, a lover. She was sure such a combination of qualities would enable her to unburden her mind and spirit of pent-up, gnawing guilt. She hoped that such a confessor would tell her to work it out in her own way. Why did she want to confess her sins? Except for persons hypersensitive and exploited by hot-gospel revivalists, isn't guilt disappearing from human beings? Isn't sin an outworn concept? The answer is that often we experience guilt because we are guilty. Certainly no one has any right to induce a sense of guilt in another. Agreed, too, that situations demand a prophetic voice to make us feel guilty about injustice in our cities, neglect of the basic needs of children, continued involvement in war.

2) Guilt-edged living is living under a burden which can become intolerable. Guilt-edged living is not the free, abundant life God intends all his children to enjoy. How to get rid of the burden? Honest and complete confession, however painful, is a primary condition for realizing forgiveness. "Father," said the younger of the two prodigals in Jesus' matchless story, "Father, I have sinned against God and against you." Restitution? Yes, when restitution is possible. Being ourselves forgiving of those who have wronged us? Jesus makes that prerequisite to realizing

* *The Waiting Father* (New York: Harper & Row, 1959).

† *Horns and Halos in Human Nature* (Old Tappan: Fleming H. Revell Company, 1954).

God's forgiveness. Said Jesus: "This is what you should pray, '. . . Forgive us our sins, / For we forgive everyone who has done us wrong' " (Luke 11:2, 4).

3) It takes courage and grace to ask forgiveness of a human being and of God. Carl Sandburg provides a moving, true account of President Lincoln's greatness of spirit. After brushing aside the plea of a Colonel Scott that he be granted leave to attend to the burial of his wife who had been accidentally drowned off Hampton Roads, Lincoln came to Scott's hotel room. "I have had a regretful night," he told the astonished officer, "and come now to beg your forgiveness."* Lincoln, who meanwhile had arranged for the permit, took the bereaved man in his own carriage to the steamship wharf and wished him godspeed.

4) Only God can provide the forgiveness we need for being wrong, as well as for doing wrong. Somehow there are resources in the universe, in the God disclosed in Christ, for absorbing our sins, for bridging the gap between the "is" and the "ought." Like the honest tax collector in Jesus' parable, when we go the way of repentance and confession we are "justified"—accepted, pardoned, restored.

## Would you believe—six?

TEXT: (*Luke 17:15, 16; 1 John 1:9; 1 Timothy 2:1; Matthew 7:7; Romans 12:1; Isaiah 6:3*).

In our "slanguage," at least as English is spoken in North America, we have a phrase usually evoking a smile: "Would you believe? . . ." In the delightful dialogue between God and Gabriel written by Richard Gilbert on the "death of God" theologians, God asks (in the manner of "De Lawd" in Marc Connelly's *The Green Pastures*), "Gabe, how many of these young Turks who say I am dead are there?" Gabe answers, "Would you believe—three?" †

Without meeting the obligation to apply the Gospel to social issues, the church offers specific opportunity and encouragement to attend to our own spiritual resources and in-

* *Lincoln: The War Years*, 4 volumes (New York: Harcourt, Brace & World, Inc., 1940), vol. 1, p. 514.

† "Dr. Altizer's Incredible Discovery" in *Presbyterian Life*, May 15, 1966.

terior life. Among the tremendously valuable resources is prayer. An open and honest seeker may ask, "What should we do in our prayers?" The Bible, the church throughout the centuries, and the experience of those who were "happy seekers and happy finders" give clear answer. Would you believe—six things we ought to do and can do in our prayers? The scripture passages listed above indicate and support these basic elements and actions and attitudes in our personal and corporate prayer.

1) *Adoration.* We adore the infinite and eternal God for himself. Said poet Joyce Kilmer at the climax of his brief, impassioned prayer of thanksgiving, "And, oh, thank God for God!" Adoration is the purest form of prayer. We find the seraphim engaged in it, and "all the company of heaven," and we, too, adore the Creator, Sustainer, Redeemer, Lord of all life.

2) *Thanksgiving.* This is the most characteristic note of Christian prayer. The majority of the healed lepers in the Lucan story took Christ and his gifts for granted. Do we? When we count our blessings, says the old hymn, we are to "name them one by one." It is the shortest, surest way to happiness, said William Law years ago. Consider the prayer of General Thanksgiving.

3) *Confession.* An examined life is the only healthy life. We are to be specific. No "Protestant incense," which you may remember Hal Luccock defined as "swinging the generalities." Be honest, be detailed, be definite in telling God sins of omission and commission, the gross ones and the sins of social attitude and action.

4) *Intercession.* This is the most unselfish kind of prayer. We are members of the church, the royal priesthood of God in our world. We come to God not just for ourselves but for others. Someone defined intercessory prayer as "prayer with names in it." For individuals, for those carrying heavy responsibilities, for those in military service, for conscientious objectors, for the sick, the rejected, the lonely, the victims of our inhumanity, for our brothers and sisters in danger and difficulty for Christ's cause, we pray. Christ makes intercession for us, and we intercede for all whom he loves.

5) *Petition or supplication.* Our Lord said, "Ask, and it will be given you." Of course, conditions are attached. We may not ask for that which is contrary to God's will as we discern this in Christ. But, as Thomas Aquinas said, whatever it is right

to ask for it is right to pray for. What we should pray for more than for "things" are the flowers and the fruits of the Spirit.

6) *Dedication.* This might be described as submission to God as his willing instruments and agents. Said William Law, "Devotion signified a life given or devoted to God." We pray truly when we offer ourselves to God that we may be his willing responsive instruments. ". . . by God's mercy . . . offer your very selves to him" (Romans 12:1, N.E.B.).

## God trusts you

TEXT: "*Before he left, he called his ten servants and gave them each a gold coin and told them, 'See what you can earn with this while I am gone'* " (*Luke 19:13* T.E.V.).

An unflattering gibe was directed at former President Charles de Gaulle of France. Allegedly circulated in France by his critics who thought he suffered from a Jehovah (or Yahweh) complex, it related the General's first morning prayer each day. Looking upward, he is supposed to save said, "Trust me, Lord!" The cruel implication is that God's world and work were being managed quite well without divine help.

Actually, say our scriptures, God does trust not only those with "kingly power" in the seats of the mighty, but all his children who respond to him with their trust and obedience. In the Parable of the Pounds as told by Luke we have probably what may be called the story of the prince royal who went abroad to seek a kingdom. It reads like the true story of Herod the Great's son Archelaus and the Jews of Judea, as told by Josephus. Most New Testament scholars prefer the counterpart of Matthew (Matthew 25:14–30). But in Luke's account we do get the truth that God (the king) trusts us his servants. He gives us resources and leaves us to use them as best we can. He does not stand over us to watch how we manage the trust or in any way interfere with our operations. One has said, "The nicest thing about God is that he trusts us to do so much by ourselves."

"Occupy till I come" is the old translation. Doubtless the more recent versions are more accurate: "See what you can earn with this while I am gone."

Our message could follow these guidelines: (1) God

trusts us to be responsible members of the family. (2) God tests us. Not merely in crises but in the way we handle the routine jobs. Think of Jesus and the thirty years out of a possible thirty-three that he spent in Nazareth. Had he not been faithful in the shop where he worked, would he have been given the supreme task of being the world's Savior? (3) God rewards us by giving us greater responsibility. God acknowledges a test well passed with more trust. (4) God trusts, tests, rewards, and tries to show us that what we do not use we lose. Advance or regress in the service of Christ; there is no permanent resting place, no final effort this side of heaven. An illustration of God's trust in us may be recalled from A. J. Cronin's novel, *The Keys of the Kingdom*. "I still can't believe in God," says the dying physician who gave his life for others in an epidemic in China. Responds the priest, "Does that matter now? He believes in you." *

## Morning! noon! and night!

TEXT: *"If you only knew today what is needed for peace!" (Luke 19:42, T.E.V.).*

"On this great day" so much happened; so much might have happened that would have made for the peace and welfare of the city and nation Jesus loved. Eyewitnesses, observers who had been present during the strange invasion by this strange King, would remember the experiences engendered by the events of morning, noon, and night.

1) In the morning they watched this unorthodox Messiah ride into the city. They were, says Dr. R. E. O. White, "rebuked by the divine lowliness." Unarmed, escorted by peasants and children, riding on what a British playwright called "a ruddy donkey," his majesty was that of meekness. Have we understood these 1900 years later that authority needs no fanfare, that truth can speak quietly, that greatness can afford to be ignored?

2) At noon the disciples had stood with their Master on the hill's crest looking over Jerusalem. They would never forget that Jesus wept over the city he loved. The city that rejected him would itself be rejected. Cities and nations seem by some dia-

* (Boston: Little, Brown and Company, 1941), pp. 211, 212.

bolical perverseness to choose their own doom. God's judgment, like that of Jesus, is not that of wrath but of compassion. We twentieth-century Christians find it hard to talk of justice and love together.

3) Night. Was there ever such a day? In the evening the dramatic challenge by Jesus of the powerful ecclesiastical authorities in their own place of business, the temple! Behold the severity and goodness of God-in-a-human-life. The Holy One demands holiness, wholesomeness. Vital religion is inseparably linked with ethics. Humility, compassion, wholeness—do these not belong to our peace too?

## "You are in good hands"

TEXT: *"Father! In your hands I place my spirit!"* (*Luke 23: 46, T.E.V.*).

The pastor stands beside the woman in the hospital room. She is a patient awaiting major surgery on the morrow. Quietly trying to reassure her, he finds that she strengthens his own confidence in the One whose presence and healing he would mediate. "I'm really not afraid," she says. "I am in good hands." Yes, the good hands of a competent surgeon, a skillful physician, a devoted nurse. But she also meant the hands of God. These words of Jesus we usually associate with Jesus' last hours, since they formed his last prayer on the cross whereon he died. Nevertheless, it was a bedtime prayer taught by devout Jewish mothers. Undoubtedly, Jesus had learned the brief "going home" prayer at Mary's knee. It is a good prayer at any time in any situation.

Professor H. George Anderson of Lutheran Theological Southern Seminary, Columbia, South Carolina, in a sermon on "Happiness or the Hand of God" used effectively the illustration of the sculptor Rodin's two small statues. Rodin called one "The Hand of the Devil," and the other, "The Hand of God." One is smoothly polished marble. It shows a cupped hand cradling a human figure. The figure lies peacefully inert. But this figure of serenity Rodin named "The Hand of the Devil." "The Hand of God" shows stone rough from the quarry, but "thrusting upward from its center is a powerful hand which seems to cleave the marble with its motion. In its grip this hand also has a human figure, carrying it upward out of unconsciousness into life." *

So, when we are in the hands of God, in the grasp of divine power and love, (1) we find frequently that to be in God's hands is to experience turbulence, a shaking-up, not placidity or unbroken peace. But "He's got the whole world in his hands," and you and me, brother, sister, in his strong hands. (2) To place ourselves and our dear ones, our church, our country, the cause of human justice and reconciliation in God's keeping is to be assured of cosmic support for what is God's purpose. With God what should be shall be. We put our hands into his hands and know that in the end truth and freedom, justice and kindness must prevail. Was it not from within the hands of God that Dr. Martin Luther King, Jr., gained the assurance that he had climbed the mountain and knew that the promised land would be entered by all God's children? (3) We are in good hands when everything else seems breaking, including our own hearts. An eminent university professor lost the wife he loved. With stunning suddenness she was gone. He wrote to an intimate friend that while the agony and finality of her death hit him with sharp impact, and that he found himself able to accept the fact of physical death, he had made another tremendous discovery. To quote his words: "It was as if a great hand was supporting my chin above the waters, holding me up."

## You do not walk alone

TEXT: "*Jesus himself drew near and walked along with them*" (*Luke 24:15, T.E.V.*). "*So then, you Gentiles are not foreigners or strangers any longer* [*outsiders, exiles, migrants and aliens, excluded from the rights of citizens*]; *you are now fellow-citizens with God's people, and members of the family of God!*" (*Ephesians 2:19*).

You do not walk alone. Many persons would strongly disagree. Since parents or husband or wife or closest friend died, they walk and live alone. But Christ's Good News affirms that man's loneliness may be God's opportunity.

1) You do not walk alone as you realize your oneness

* *Renewal in the Pulpit*, ed. Edmund A. Steimle (Philadelphia: Fortress Press, 1966), pp. 65, 66.

with other members of the human race. See 1 Samuel 25:29 (R.S.V.) for a memorable phrase describing this fact of existence. We are "bound in the bundle of the living in the care of the Lord." To join the human race requires an act of will, a deep interest in the concern for others—and God's grace.

2) You need never walk alone, because you have God for your friend. A thoughtful reader of Alfred North Whitehead's famous dictum that religion is what we do with our solitariness suggested that it sounds even truer to say, "what one does with solitariness is religion." Jesus Christ came to create community and to call men into community—the dynamic, transforming community of God's love. For untold numbers of people the last chapter of Luke's Gospel is fact: "Jesus himself drew near and went with them."

Simone Weil (1909–43) was led to direct experience of God and singularly complete devotion to Christ although she never received Christian baptism. In one of her books she tells how "Christ himself came down and took possession of me." She was reciting George Herbert's poem "Love" at the time. "I only felt in the midst of my suffering the presence of a love, like that which one can read in the smile of a beloved face." *

Christ's affirmation has been tested and found true: "Lo, I am with you—always." How do they know the companionship of the living Lord? As Bernard of Clairvaux said eight centuries ago, by the renovation and reformation of mind and spirit.

3) We experience God's friendship in Christ within the community of his friends we call the church. In this community we are given release from the prison of the moment and from the jail of our solitariness into the unbroken communion of saints. As the Apostle is saying to the Christians in the young church of Ephesus, you are no longer in the church on a tourist's passport, nor among God's people on a kind of alien resident's visa. You are full citizens of God's kingdom, members of his family.

"Fellow citizens with the saints" may not be too appealing even to a gregarious modern soul. Said the boy, "I don't want to be a saint; I want to be a real guy." But the meaning

* *Waiting on God* (New York: G. P. Putnam's Sons, 1959) pp. 24, 25.

of "saint" in the New Testament is "a real guy": a person whole, complete—at least on the way to completion. A saint is one who has given himself away to Jesus Christ and all for whom Christ died. A saint is a Christian on the road to Christlikeness. We are in the most ecumenical society in the world. The good and great, the "little people" and the obscure are in it with us, cheering us on and—who knows?—perhaps helping us on toward the city of God.

And there is always Christ.

## "More light than we can learn"

TEXT: "*The light shines in the darkness, and the darkness has never put it out. . . . This was the real light, the light that comes into the world and shines on all men*" (*John 1:5, 9, T.E.V.*).

Orson Welles' realistic radio play based on the H. G. Wells science fiction story of outer space warriors invading our planet filled thousands of radio listeners in the 1930s with panic. Filled with dread they rushed into the streets fearing destruction by mythical militants. Only repeated, nationwide reassurance that it was a play and not a newscast allayed the dread. Simple, sturdy men guarding their sheep and lambs in Judean hills on the first Christmas night were filled with something resembling those feelings of dread. Read Luke 2:8–12 for the effect of the strange invasion of the earth through the birth of Jesus. "They were terribly afraid," reported Luke. The heavenly messenger—the angel—reassured them: "Don't be afraid! For I am here with good news for you, which will bring great joy to all people. This very night in David's town your Savior was born—Christ the Lord!" Using philosophical language current at the time he wrote, John describes the superhuman character of the One who came as a baby in Bethlehem. Jesus, he declares, is the Word, the divine Reason behind and within and through and over all things. Then he uses one of his favorite figures of speech, "This was the real light, the light that comes into the world and shines on all men." This is the inextinguishable light: "The light shines in the darkness, and the darkness has never put it out."

## [76] "More light than we can learn"

Twentieth-century poet-playwright Christopher Fry of England expressed the significance of the coming of Christ in these lines:

*The darkest night of the year,*
*The poorest place in town,*
*Cold, and a taste of fear,*
*Man and woman alone . . .*
*What can we hope for here?*
*More light than we can learn,*
*More wealth than we can treasure,*
*More love than we can earn,*
*More peace than we can measure,*
*Because one child is born.*

Think of that first consequence of Christ's "invasion" of our human territory. "Because one child is born" and this child Jesus, born of Mary, because he grew to manhood, worked, taught, preached, healed, was killed while still a young man, and was raised from the dead, we have more light, more truth, more insight than we can learn. Light is a symbol of truth, of knowledge. We have "more light than we can learn," more than we can grasp, (1) on the mystery of life. In this baby who became man, the mind of God, the eternal's purpose and nature were disclosed, personalized. "For what is life?" asks Paul in his letter to Philippian Christians. He answers: "To me, it is Christ!" (Philippians 1:21). (2) We have "more light than we can learn on our own identity and value." ". . . we are now God's children . . . " affirms the scripture (1 John 3:2).

Of course man in his time and in his moods is many things. We are kin to the lower animals. Who has not exhibited traits of the tiger, the ape, the monkey, the mule? We are physical, but more. Gladly we acknowledge our physical hungers and drives. We can also think and plan and dream. We are children of the great God; are we not made in his spiritual likeness? Because we are God's children we ought to live like them in our relationships to others in his family. Our value is infinitely more than we place upon ourselves or others estimate in low moods. Christ thought us worth dying for to redeem. (3) We have "more light" on our duty and upon our destiny. Because Christ illumines what life is about, and who we are, and what we may become, we must live a life of intelligent, invincible benevolence toward ourselves and toward all others. As for our destiny, our Lord was sure it was unlimited. Our true life is eternal and therefore unbroken by bodily death. The little girl's account of the Sunday church school's lesson on Enoch is worth recalling. "There was this man Enoch. He went for walks with God. One was especially long and God said to him 'Enoch you must be tired. Come in and rest.' " It is a sound interpretation of the verse, "And Enoch walked with God; and he was not, for God took him" (Genesis 5:24 R.S.V.).

## Who cares for Christmas?

TEXT: *"The Word became a human being and lived among us. We saw his glory, full of grace and truth. This was the glory which he received as the Father's only Son"* (*John 1:14, T.E.V.*).

1) Manufacturers, department store owners, merchants care for Christmas. They love the music of cash registers and computers working on charge accounts at the time when millions buy gifts.

2) Children and grownups with childlike hearts care greatly for Christmas.

3) Those who found newness of life in Christ care deeply for the Christ of Christmas. He broke the power of ruinous habits for them. He opened the gates of new life to them.

4) Some could not care less. It was always so. "He came to his own, and his own received him not." There are still heedless crowds, self-sufficient descendants of the Bethlehem innkeeper. The exploiters of human weakness hate Christmas. But in the words of a carol, "Ask the saved of all the race / Who have found his favor." They will tell you how much they care that Christmas, or rather the Christ who made Christmas, has come to our world.

How much do we care? Enough to kneel in loving loyalty to the Lord who came as a "tiny baby thing" and was laid on the doorstep of the world? Do we care enough to "enlist for the duration" in Christ's Peace Corps? As the divine Word became a human being in Jesus on the first Christmas, so the divine Word must take flesh in our personalities and be incarnate in the living church, his body, at last to be embodied in the world of men.

## Making water into wine

TEXT: "*They took it [the water] to him [the steward or master of ceremonies at the wedding reception], and he tasted the water which had turned into wine*" (*John* 2:8, *T.E.V.*).

Did Jesus actually turn ordinary water into wine, the kind of wine which elicited exclamations of delight? Sure that the story is literally true, C. S. Lewis argued that the God who through the natural order can turn water, soil, and sunshine plus grapes into a juice that under proper conditions can become wine, could, through Christ, shorten the process. But John seems concerned about something else, something more than miracle. This is a "sign," he is saying, a sign of the glory of God's Kingdom. Jesus spoke of the new wine of the kingdom (Mark 2:10–22). Into the insipid religious life of his people Jesus brought the active ferment of a new message and a new power. It is Christ who makes the difference. (a) Christ turns the brackish, bitter water of guilt into the wine of God's pardon. "Come to me," he says in the power of the Spirit, "and I will give you forgiveness and newness of life." (b) Christ changes the water of dull existence into joy-filled living. There is joy within the Father's house. God says to his children what Harry Golden is sure life says: "Enjoy! Enjoy!" (c) Christ longs to change the water of sorrow into his wine of comfort and courage. "Are you with me, Lord?" we ask with Moses in Marc Connelly's play *Green Pastures*. We too may feel one beside us saying, "Of course I am. I am with you always." (d) Christ comes and transforms the emptiness of life into fullness of life by making us sure of God's love and by making us able to love and to be loved. We know God as we learn to love. "Whoever does not love does not know God, because God is love" (1 John 4:8).

When the first Christians heard and read this story of the Cana wedding attended by Jesus and his mother and his disciples they thought of the Lord's Supper. In that sacrament they found contact with the unseen, living Lord. He made all the difference. For where he touched their spirits they experienced God's own touch, and when they welcomed him he turned the water of life into the best of wine.

## How one man matured

TEXT: "*There was a man named Nicodemus, a leader of the Jews, who belonged to the party of the Pharisees. One night he came to Jesus . . .* (*John 3:1, T.E.V.*). *Nicodemus was one of them; he was the one who had gone to see Jesus before. He said to them . . .*" (*John 7:50*). *Nicodemus, who at first had gone to see Jesus at night, went with Joseph, taking with him about one hundred pounds of spices, a mixture of myrrh and aloes*" (*John 19:39*).

A Canadian theologian preacher of an earlier generation, the late Dr. Robert Laws, had a sermon on this interesting personality. Here were his divisions: (1) Nicodemus the cautious inquirer; (2) Nicodemus the diplomatic advocate; (3) Nicodemus the convinced confessor.

## Let's celebrate!

TEXT: "*God loved the world so much . . .*" (*John 3:16, T.E.V.*).

Renewal of the church is a major concern of Christians of all branches of the community of Christ. From time to time our prophetic leaders urge us to make top priority the renewal of the world. "A renewed church for a renewed world" may be more than a slogan; it may be the call of God himself. In the Old Testament book of Zechariah we have a mystic who for some two years (520–518 B.C.) encouraged the builders of the temple to renew their world. He puts heart into them with his visions of the messianic kingdom that was about to come. Vividly he sketches a picture of what the city and temple will be like when the exiles have returned. Old people and children would be secure, happy, contented. In verse 19 of chapter eight he declares that even the commemorations of tragic events shall be to God's people occasions for celebration: "joy and gladness, and cheerful feasts."

The Lord's Supper commemorates the most tragic event in history: the judicial murder of the fairest and best, the Son of God. Often the solemnity of the sacrifice of Jesus makes us subdued, sad, even somber. Yet this is the feast, the fast of Christ's appointing, and he came and died and rose again, he said, that his joy might be complete in us. Let's celebrate!

In some churches this service is designated a celebration of Holy Communion, of the Eucharist, of the Lord's Supper. What do we celebrate?

1) We celebrate a love, the greatest love. As *Today's English Version* renders the gospel within the gospel, John 3:16: "For God loved the world so much that he gave his only Son, so that everyone who believes in him may not die but have eternal life." "Love so amazing, so divine" demands not only all that we are and have, but evokes our joy in heartiest gratitude. For his love means that we are forgiven.

2) We celebrate a victory. Ours is not a dead hero but a living and reigning Lord. Over Jesus Christ death had no power (Romans 6:9). "Christ must rule" (1 Corinthians 15:25). He occupies the territory of this world, and V-Day will come, within or beyond history.

3) We celebrate a Presence. "I will come back to you," he promised (John 14:18). He has kept his promise. He comes quietly, decisively, though the doors are shut, to those who give him their trust, love, obedience. We who belong to the reformed branch of the great church believe in the real spiritual presence of Christ in the sacrament. It is more than a Founder's feast, a commemoration; it is a communion.

4) We celebrate a fellowship. Said the editor of a religious weekly to a colleague who left the journal for another position: "Remember the *koinonia*." In your new field, recall the friendship we enjoyed in our job here, was his meaning. We remember the *koinonia*; we experience the companionship with Christ and one another in this service. Let's celebrate!

5) We celebrate a promotion. We are promoted by God's grace mediated to us through his living presence in our worship, from pedestrian to purposeful living, from despair to hope, from apathy to adventures in our world whereby the world itself shall be remade.

## Giant leap for mankind

TEXT: "*For God loved the world so much that he gave his only Son, so that everyone who believes in him may not die but have eternal life*" (*John 3:16, T.E.V.*).

On our first "Moonday," Sunday, July 20, 1969, the astronaut Neil Armstrong placed man's first footprint on the moon at 10:56 P.M. As he cautiously did so, he declared: "That's one small step for man, one giant leap for mankind." When Jesus of Nazareth was born of Mary in Bethlehem it was truly a giant leap for man and for mankind. The poet had insight when he said long before the Space Age arrived, "God may have other words for other worlds, but the Word of God for this world is Christ." The divine Word, the ultimate reality, became a human being in Jesus Christ as in no other person. Only God could have dreamed of this invasion of planet Earth. Only God could have met our deepest needs by becoming "very man of very man." Think of the giant leap (1) toward true manhood, true womanhood. "The Son of God," said an early Church leader, "became the son of man that the sons of men might become the sons of God." (2) toward freedom from sin with its guilt and despair. The Good News of John 3:16 is completed in John 3:17—"For God did not send his Son into the world to be its Judge, but to be its Savior." Man may visit many planets, but always he must come back to earth. On earth as anywhere in the cosmos man must master himself, learn to accept himself, learn to live as a member of God's human family. Christ saves "everyone who believes in him" *from* the power of evil and saves "everyone who believes in him" *into* a life of joy, peace, usefulness. (3) Because God loved the world so much he gave his only Son to live, to teach and act as he did, to die on the Cross, and to rise from the dead to live forever with and among his own, "everyone who believes in him" has taken a "giant leap" over and through physical and spiritual death. Eternal life is life in its depth, its height, its breadth, and in its illimitable length. Eternal life begins here and now. It is a new dimension of living. "And this *is* eternal life," Jesus affirmed (John 17:3) "for men to know you, the only true God, and to know Jesus Christ, whom you sent." Eternal life means life beyond death and the grave. "Actually," wrote Paul to fellow Christians, "everything belongs to you . . .

this world, life and death, the present and the future; all of these are yours, and you belong to Christ, and Christ belongs to God" (1 Corinthians 3:21–23).

## "Enclosed by arms not of this world"

TEXT: *"For God did not send his Son into the world to be its Judge, but to be its Savior" (John 3:17, T.E.V.).*

An eminent Christian leader of our time is the Reverend Dr. Helmut Thielicke of Hamburg, Germany, who is considered to be one of Europe's most popular preachers. He relates the story of his kneeling in the prairie sand of South West Africa, celebrating the Lord's Supper with some Herero tribesmen. Listen to Dr. Thielicke:

"They had never heard of our city, and I had known nothing of that remote bush country 'where the deer and the antelope play.' Neither of us understood a single word of the other's language. But when I made the sign of the cross with my hand and pronounced the name 'Jesus,' their dark faces lit up. We ate the same bread and drank from the same chalice, despite apartheid, and they couldn't do enough to show me their love. They held out their children to me and took me into their poor huts. We had never seen each other before. We were separated by social, geographical, and cultural barriers. And yet we were enclosed by arms that were not of this world. Then the scales fell from my eyes; I began to understand the story of Pentecost. I understood the miracle of the Church.

"We were enclosed by arms that were not of this world." *

(1) Whose arms? The Arms of God, the arms of God's dear Son Jesus Christ once outstretched upon the Cross of Calvary. The Bible declares that "underneath are the everlasting arms." It is a lovely way of saying that supporting every one of us, every one of God's children, is eternal love, the love that will never let us go however low we sink in sin, or weakness, or despair. We—each of us—are "enclosed by arms that are not of this world." As the spiritual sings it, "He's got the whole world in his hands."

* *I Believe,* trans. J. W. Doberstein and H. G. Anderson (Philadelphia: Fortress Press, 1968), p. 231.

(2) As the great German preacher declared, this is the only way we can understand the miracle of the Church. The Church, with all its faults, its self-centered and "little members," is the hope of the world. Why? One tremendous reason is that it is the Lord's own creation and concern. "The gates of Hell—the powers of darkness—shall not prevail against her," because it is enclosed, protected, loved by God himself. It—more accurately—we are "enclosed by arms that are not of this world." On Worldwide Communion Sunday the Holy Communion symbolizes this love, this unity, this power. In this Sacrament partaken together we experience the miracle of God's presence and caring.

(3) Once more, thinking of what the Bread and Wine represent, of the divine Presence and Grace they convey, we realize anew what our response must be. You and I are "enclosed by arms not of this world" in order to do what? In order that we may enclose the world—at least that part we can reach by our actions, by our prayers, by our money—with something of Christ's transforming love.

A little girl, twirling a globe, found America and kissed it, and then she put her arms around the entire globe. That is what a strong church such as ours does: We love and serve in our community and nation but we never forget the wider world. Jesus said, "It was not to judge the world that God sent His Son into the world, but that through Him the world might be saved" (John 3:17, N.E.B.). AMEN.

## When we fear the light

TEXT: "*This is how the judgment works: the light has come into the world, but men love the darkness rather than the light, because they do evil things. And anyone who does evil things hates the light and will not come to the light, because he does not want his evil deeds to be shown up*" (*John 3:19–21, T.E.V.*).

Following devastating floods in the winter of 1967, citizens of Florence, Italy, awaited Midsummer Day with anxiety. Why? Because of what the light in their magnificent medieval cathedral might reveal. Embedded in the floor directly beneath the towering dome is an inconspicuous brass plate. Its importance is vital. Once every year, on June 22, a solitary sunbeam filters down through a hole high in the vaulted roof and gleams on the brass plate, illuminating it for a moment. Over five centuries ago the architects so designed the dome that any deviation of the midsummer shaft of sunlight would give warning that the structure had shifted on its foundations. Annually ever since, the light has proclaimed the truth about the soundness of the foundations. Following the severe floods, the Florentines kept anxious watch for what might have been a fateful verdict of the light.

1) Florence's ancient cathedral may be a long distance in space and time from the church you attend. Yet in every Christian congregation the unfailing Light shines. That light, as John's Gospel declares, is Christ. God in Christ is light: the light of truth, of justice, of love. "The Word had life in himself, and this life brought light to men" (John 1:4). Wherever the gospel of Christ is proclaimed, wherever two or three or many more keep their appointment with the living Lord in worship, whenever we confront Christ in person-to-person encounter, the Light judges us.

2) This judgment by the light of God in Jesus Christ penetrates to the foundations. It does not just play over the surface of our person and social life. This can be uncomfortable, disturbing, and to some persons unbearable. Like Simon Peter when he saw his Master coming toward him, a person is apt to cry, "Go away; depart from me, for I am a sinful man, O Lord!" Nevertheless, no radical change can take place in an individual or a community until we honestly face up to the unpleasant truth about ourselves. Said a psychiatrist about a fine young couple who were sure a change of location and even vocation might be the cure of their difficulties. "They are unwilling, perhaps because they are not yet sufficiently mature, to face up to something basically wrong in their marriage relationship." The Reverend Nelson Gray of the Church of Scotland, to whom I am indebted for the true story of the cathedral in Florence, wonders if this may be a reason "why so many give Christ's church a miss." (That is British slang for nonattendance at worship.) Is it, he wonders, because "beyond all the excuses, they are afraid of the searching verdict of the Light that never fails"?

3) When we overcome our fear of the light of Christ judging us, we not only see plainly how wrong we have been, and how shifty and shifting our foundations, but we see the Light of

the World in all his love and forgiveness. In verse 18 of John 3 (N.E.B.) is the great assurance: "The man who puts his faith in him does not come under judgement." And in verse 21: "The honest man comes to the light so that it may be clearly seen that God is in all he does."

## If I should die before I live

TEXT: "*. . . the time is coming—the time has already come—when the dead will hear the voice of the Son of God, and those who hear it will live*" (*John 5:25*, T.E.V.).

Some adults may recall the bedtime prayer, "Now I lay me down to sleep, I pray the Lord my soul to keep; if I should die before I wake, I pray the Lord my soul to take." Christian educators and some child psychologists frown upon such a prayer because of the emphasis on death. However, there is a more disturbing thought than the possibility of death overtaking us during sleep. What if we should die before we live? True, in most human beings the will to live remains stronger than the so-called death wish. A poet spoke for most human beings when he said:

*'Tis life whereof our nerves are scant,*
*Oh, life, not death, for which we pant;*
*More life, and fuller, that we want.*
*Sir Walter Scott* (*1771–1832*)

Occasionally newspapers report the sad plight of individuals who exist following some serious accident or illness, but outside of breathing, pulse, and heartbeat, there is little indication of living as we understand and value it. Isn't it possible for many persons not so afflicted to exist in God's world of beauty, color, vast possibilities for service to others, and make no positive response?

John's Gospel shows us Jesus as the life-giver, the restorer of life to those literally dead. The word also may be used of those spiritually, morally and emotionally dead. Consider:

1) You and I are dying before we truly live when we give up trying. If we accept ourselves as finished products, we are finished. If we surrender to any kind of fatalism that our faults and failures are inescapable and beyond redemption,

we are already dying. But Christ came that everyone might have a second chance, and a third, and yet another. No person needs to remain half-dead or hopeless. Phyllis McGinley drew a picture of a life content with minimum existence in her book *Occupation: Housewife*. Its message merits careful reading. Jesus said to his contemporaries what he says to many of us now: "Yet you are not willing to come to me in order to have life" (John 5:40). In his company, serving causes which he must desire to have advanced, we get busy living from a great depth of being.

2) People die before they really live when they have no sense of direction, no chosen and commanding goal. Sometimes young people suspect that we older persons have this deficiency. Said one high school student to another about a third brilliant student: "No wonder he's good in French. His father and mother talk French at home all the time." Said the other, "Then I ought to be good in geometry, my parents talk in circles all the time." When we move in circles with no significant goal, we are already living at a "poor dying rate." Said our Lord in words which hit us with powerful impact still: ". . . give first place to his Kingdom and to what he requires, and he will provide you with all these other things." To the rich young society leader he gave the directive to love God and his neighbor with all he had and was, and added, "This do and you will live."

3) If I should die before I wake up and live it may be due to my willingness to settle for the most minimal faith. At a campaign for hospital funds a high-powered fund raiser told the canvassers: "Never suggest to any prospective giver a sum as a minimum contribution. For a minimum contribution has a funny way of turning into a maximum."

Do we settle for a minimum of Christian faith and conviction? No one wants a maximum of impossible beliefs. Our Lord placed no premium on credulousness. A vital faith is one that goes to the depth of life and lives in scorn of consequences. Read John 5:24. Said a gallant woman novelist named Ann Douglas Sedgwich during a long, crippling illness: "Life is a queer struggle. Yet, it is mine, and beautiful to me. There is joy in knowing I lie in the hands of God." Do you not sense that while dying she was living greatly?

4) If I should die before I live it will be because I refuse to give myself away. "He that loses his life for my sake," said

the Master of life and of the art of living, "shall find it." When we know that God cares for us and for all his children so much that he gave the Son of his love to die for us, then we start caring. To start caring, to keep on caring for and about others, is to begin living. When we get the icicles of apathy and self-centeredness off our hearts, warm, pulsating new life surges through.

## Think small! Think big!

TEXT: ". . . *But what good are they for all these people?*" (*John 6:9, T.E.V.*). "*For who hath despised the day of small things?*" (*Zechariah 4:10, K.J.V.*).

1) Thinking small is generally condemned, unless you are selling a popular imported small car. A recent cartoon showed a Volkswagen dealer saying to a salesman, "Think big and you're fired!" Thinking small has cursed too many politicians, churchmen, and upholders of the status quo. Nevertheless, it is true that contempt for the small, for the few, for the weak, has also blighted the human situation and even hindered the growth of the Christian cause.

Christ's first followers naturally took a dim view of a few loaves and fishes in a boy's picnic lunch. "What are they among so many?" Their evaluation proved wrong. Given to meet human need the meager lunch fed the multitude. Whether the miracle took place in the loaves and fishes or in the minds and spirits of the crowd is not particularly important at this time. Americans and Canadians (and probably others) have been guilty of being champions of what was once called the cult of Jumboism, worship of the biggest elephant. Recall the response of Jesus to the disciples' admiration for the big size of the Jerusalem temple (Mark 13:1, 2).

A distinguished contemporary preacher, the Very Reverend Angus J. MacQueen of Toronto, Canada, once preached an effective stewardship sermon on the Zechariah text. He urged his hearers not to despise the world of small opportunities and situations, the "little person," the ordinary human being, and the local congregation of the Great Church. In Advent and at Christmas we adore God-in-a-human-life who came as a "tiny baby thing" in a small town in an obscure province of the Roman Empire. His human parents were from the "little people." But the child grew to manhood and became the world's most powerful instrument for the transformation of individuals and nations.

2) "Think big!" is also a word of God to us. Cecil Rhodes in what is now South Africa may have been a ruthless exploiter of human beings as he amassed his fortune. He is remembered, at least by the almost extinct species once known as British empire builders, for his vision of what small communities might become. "Use large maps!" was a frequent directive he issued. As Christians in a world shrinking through technological advance, we must "think big"; we must think of the whole world and not just of our own private domain. "God loved the world so much," says John's Gospel (3:16, N.E.B.). " . . . the field is the world," said Jesus (Matthew 13:38). Do we not as Christ's men and women pledge allegiance to his cause in one world, under God, indivisible, with liberty, justice, and love for all?

Thinking big with Christian vision and insight includes thinking with something more than "hear the pennies dropping" for the support of Christ's cause; something more than thinking of just a few radical agitators when we think of city ghettos and a large minority group needs; something more than settling for the local church's program, budget, ministry in the world.

## How words can change the world

TEXT: "*What gives life is the Spirit; the flesh is of no use at all. The words I have spoken to you are Spirit and life*" (*John 6:63, T.E.V.*).

The late Senator Everett Dirksen of Illinois once said, "The reason I keep my words soft, honeyed, and warm, is because I never know when I may be called upon to eat them." Soon or late each of us has to eat words we have spoken, whether sweet or sour. These words are in the form of promises, pledges, assertions. We make them to ourselves, to each other, to God.

In John's sixth chapter, Jesus is reported trying to interpret his teaching concerning the Lord's Supper, which even his loyal followers found hard to take. To Jesus, words were never "mere words." To devout Hebrews, the words of God meant the written law, the Torah. As someone said, a word is an external act which carries a meaning. A word of God is any expression from the divine source which transmits God's intention to us.

1) Words, being acts, are in themselves deeds, and deeds can change the world's goals, methods, character. When a man's word no longer means much, business, politics, religion suffer deeply. When Churchill spoke to his fellow countrymen and to lovers of responsible freedom everywhere in the darkest days of 1940, his words were weapons, full of "battle-hope." A vivid illustration of how a good person's encouraging words can change a young person's stance, style, and ultimately his way of living is told by Dr. Harry Emerson Fosdick in his autobiography.*

2) When we think of mind-shaping and world-changing words we must think of One whom the Christian scriptures call the Word made flesh, Jesus Christ (John 1:14). In his teachings, his life, his death, his resurrection, Jesus Christ is God's deed. When he speaks, when he acts, we sense that we hear God speaking to us in words inaudible to physical hearing. In Christ it is always "Yes" (2 Corinthians 1:19–20). For all the promises of God find their "Yes" in the Word of God personalized in Jesus Christ.

3) What words do we speak to others?—in our spoken speech? in our written words? in the word of our lives? Do our words help keep men and women on their feet in a shaking society (see Moffatt's translation of Job 4:4)? The late Rufus Jones, the Quaker philosopher and Christian saint, had a favorite word for Christians. He said that we are "transmitters." What messages are we transmitting?

## A grief observed

TEXT: (*John 11:1–44, T.E.V.*).

The late C. S. Lewis, famous British scholar, Christian, and writer, married fairly late in life. After only a few years of uncommonly happy married love, Mrs. Lewis died from a long and painful illness. Mr. Lewis began a journal—a poi-

* *The Living of These Days* (New York: Harper & Row, Publishers, 1956), pp. 65, 76.

gnant, memorable record of the thoughts of a sorely bereaved man.* From such a brief, insight-packed book, and from the One "acquainted with grief" who himself was deeply moved by his friends' grieving following their brother's death (John 11:33), we may find help to use our own grief well. It is helpful in calm weather to think about our resources when a storm strikes.

1) Christians as well as those professionally trained in the dynamics of human behavior should know that grief must work itself out. It is neither wise nor Christian to repress our deep feelings of loss, of loneliness, of guilt which sometimes are stimulated by the death of a dear one. "Jesus wept." He who knew that love need never lose its own was not too stoical, too controlled to cry. Who has not observed the delayed reaction to a death in a family by one whose apparent courage would not let him express grief at the time of the death?

2) Grief is like a physical wound and must be followed by healing. One physician who studied the grieving process listed the stages. First, there is shock and disbelief at the unexpected loss. It is hard to accept the reality of it. Next there is growing awareness of the loss. Often we feel a deep emptiness and cry the way a child cries for help. Interestingly enough, this physician found that the funeral rites or memorial service may be the first step in the healing. Friends help to alleviate the pain. A religious service which affirms the reality of physical death and also the reality of resurrection into life eternal for all who trust God plays a vital part in the healing.

3) The deepest healing is found in companionship with Christ. His assurance of the unbroken life (John 14 contains the classical affirmation) for all who put their trust in him is the assurance of one who has the authority and right to speak. His own victory over death is one we can share. Christ's people, clerical and so-called "lay," mediate Christ and his comfort. This is one of the reasons we are here.

## More than a happening

TEXT: *"Jesus said to her; 'I am the resurrection and the life. Whoever believes in me will live, even though he dies' . . ." (John 11:25, T.E.V.).*

* See *A Grief Observed* (New York: The Seabury Press, Inc., 1963).

Young people, and not just hippies and yippies, have taught older citizens the meaning of what they call a "happening." It is more than an occurrence or event to be observed objectively. When you are at, or in, a happening, you are personally involved, caught up, "with it." You may never be quite the same again. Easter commemorates a happening, but is much more than a happening of the first Christian century. Easter is the name given the mysterious, cosmic event we call Christ's resurrection from death. It is not enough to believe that the resurrection of Christ happened as the scriptures declare. We must believe not only in a past event but in a living person, the living Christ. Consider, then, the startling and unique claim of Christ when he said, "I am the resurrection and the life."

1) Because of this happening and the first disciples' experience of the risen Lord, we have the gospels, the epistles, the Acts, and the rest of the New Testament; we have the Christian Sunday; we have Christmas and Pentecost. If there had been no resurrection there would be no Christmas. Because of our confidence in Christ's living presence and action we have the living church in all its expressions.

2) Our confidence in the living Lord gives us the gospel that has changed the world in many of its areas in many of its eras, and can change the world today.

3) Christ is the resurrection and the life for all who put their trust in him. On that first Easter morning a new world was born, just as on the first Good Friday "the world had died in the night."* Although Easter does not "prove" human immortality, it does promise that all who commit themselves to Christ will have eternal life here and now and forever. He is the Lord of the living and of the dead. Where Christ is, there will his people also be.

In France, in the nineteenth century, there lived a famous tightrope walker known as Blondin. His real name was Jean François Gravelet. On one occasion, after he had carried a man on his shoulders across a great height on a tightrope before a large and spellbound crowd, a certain small boy attracted Blondin's attention. The boy was staring open-mouthed at him in awe. Said the tightrope walker to the boy: "Do you believe that I could carry you on my shoulders across that rope?" "Of course you could, sir," replied the boy. "Right, then," said

* G. K. Chesterton, *The Everlasting Man* (Garden City: Doubleday & Company, Inc., 1955), p. 13.

Blondin, "up you get on my shoulders and I'll take you across." That was something else again, and the boy would not go. There is a difference between believing that something happened, that the Resurrection somehow occurred, and trusting oneself and one's cause to the risen Lord. Have we the faith, the trust, to make the venture?

## Sunny intervals

TEXT: "*The light will be among you a little longer. Live your lives while you have the light, so the darkness will not come upon you; because the one who lives in the dark does not know where he is going*" (*John 12:35, T.E.V.*).

If you have visited the United Kingdom you have enjoyed the British Broadcasting Corporation weather forecasts. One which amuses visitors from sunnier lands speaks of the fog, or mist, or low pressures moving in from Iceland, of the frequent rain, and adds, "with sunny intervals." The scriptures of our faith are equally honest. Never does the Bible conceal the fact that cosmic weather and the climate in which human beings operate can be stormy, dark, turbulent. Always, however, the biblical meteorologists assure us there will be sunny intervals. For the Christian every day should have some radiance. True, we live in a world where the demonic powers of night often seem to be in the ascendant. Pain strikes, sorrow hits us or those we know, corruption marries prejudice and spawns a malignant brood. Clouds black out the shining of the sun of peace. Nevertheless, God is, and God rules. Christ is a fact of history and of experience.

Alistair MacLean was a Highland Scottish minister serving a little parish in the north of Scotland. He died over twenty years ago. However, his messages still bring hope and faith to those who read them in his books: *High Country, The Quiet Heart,* and *Radiant Certainty.* "The very highest kind of character depends on the weather you are having in your spirit."* In his conviction you may find emphases for your own message on this theme: (1) your moral and spiritual weather can be warm with the warmth of Christian friendship:

* *The Happy Finder* (London: Allenson and Co., Ltd., 1949), pp. 124–28.

(2) you can have the brightness of the sunshine of hope and vital faith in the God who comes near to us in Christ; (3) if you have knowledge of some work done as well as you could do it, there will be lovely weather in your spirit.

Does all this sound naïve, reminiscent of Pollyanna ("the glad girl") or the incurable and unrealistic optimist? It is a fact for men and women who are "in Christ." He is the light of the world, and he expected us to be lights in our world. Again and again, biblical writers use figures of speech to tell us of his light-giving power. He is "the sun of righteousness with healing in its wings." He is the "bright morning star." He that walks with him is in the light. "Believe in the light, then, while you have it, so that you will be the people of the light" (John 12:36).

## How to handle pride

TEXT: (*John 13:3–5; T.E.V.*).

1) Pride is the deadliest of the deadly sins. The Bible condemns it and prophesies doom for the arrogant and haughty (Proverbs 16:18). An apocryphal book—Ecclesiasticus 10:15—asserts that "pride is the beginning of sin." But why knock pride? Should not every person have a decent pride in himself? in his family? in his country? in his church? Yes, a decent, or better still, a Christian pride. But the pride condemned by both the scriptures and the church is undue conceit of ourselves. This works havoc when it expresses itself in being too proud to confess sin or failure, or in racial arrogance and racial superiority. Nations continue senseless war because one or both sides in the conflict are too proud to risk "a loss of face." Husbands and wives often wreck their marriage because one or both are too proud to admit "I was wrong. I am sorry." The late C. S. Lewis did not overstate the indictment when he wrote: "Unchastity, anger, greed, drunkenness, are mere flea bites in comparison with pride." Pride is putting self in God's place. Pride is attempting to play God.

2) What is the way to handle pride? Not by the Uriah Heep approach and attitude. Uriah said, superciliously, "I ate 'umble pie with an appetite." Christ helps us handle pride by giving us directives and an example. See Luke 14:11 and an

echo of Christ's teaching in James 4:6. John Bunyan accepted Christ's stance and said, "He that is down, needs fear no fall; he that is low, no pride; he that is humble ever shall have God to be his guide." Much more, Christ gives us his grace to be truly humble (and never proud of our humility!).

In a sermon preached in World War II, during the blitz of London, Leslie D. Weatherhead concluded with these unforgettable words, ". . . when a foul egotism rises up within me and would bid me assert myself, plan for myself, serve my own interests, play my own hand and 'take care of number one': then, O my Lord, may I hear in imagination the gentle splashing of water falling into a basin, and see the *Son of God* washing his disciples' feet!"*

## Way, truth, life

TEXT: "*I am the way, I am the truth, I am the life . . .*" (*John 14:6, T.E.V.*).

Here is a sermon outline by an unknown genius for getting to the heart of one of Jesus' tremendous sayings. (1) Without the way, there is no going. (2) Without the truth, there is no knowing. (3) Without the life, there is no growing. Can you make that the framework of a message which will let the Word "find" both preacher and hearer?

## That's the Spirit!

TEXT: (*John 14:15; 14:26; 15:26, 27*).

A Cornell University president remarked to a visiting preacher: "I have heard almost every sermon by distinguished visiting preachers, including eminent theologians, here in Sage Chapel. Not once in all these years have I heard a sermon on the Holy Spirit." Wistfully, he added, "I would like to hear one interpretation of the church's teaching on the Spirit."

Pentecost Sunday is an appropriate time to think of this doctrine. Many modern citizens resemble the Ephesians to whom Paul spoke. If you were to repeat the Apostle's question,

* *The Eternal Voice* (Nashville: Abingdon Press, 1940), pp. 73–82.

"Did you receive the Holy Spirit when you became believers?" they could honestly answer, "No . . . we have not even heard that there is a Holy Spirit" (Acts 19:2. N.E.B.). Others are confused as a result of the apparently inconsistent references to "the Holy Spirit," "the Spirit," "the Spirit of Jesus." These terms are interchangeable. Moreover, the New Testament writers are unanimous in affirming that the Holy Spirit is God at work in the world, in the lives of men, in the community of faith and redemptive love which is the church. Jesus himself prepared the first Christians for an experience of the Holy Spirit when, in one of his last conversations with them in the Upper Room, he forecast the Spirit's coming (John 14, 15, 16). The greatest missionary teacher of them all, the Apostle Paul, experienced this "One who stands beside" (the meaning of the word translated in some versions of the scriptures: "paraclete"). Early Christians soon realized that the Holy Spirit was one who had the character of Jesus. The guiding and supportive power, the tender healing action, the transforming and keeping love of Christ are available now as they were in Palestine of old. Study of the relevant chapters of John's Gospel suggests a threefold answer to the question, "Who or what is the Holy Spirit?"

1) The Spirit is the *champion* (advocate, helper; literally, someone called in to help, John 14:16). The old translation "Comforter" will do if you give the word the old meaning: one who enabled a discouraged, beaten soul to be brave. The Holy Spirit brings God into the situation as Christ did.

2) The Spirit is the *instructor* ("the Holy Spirit whom the Father will send in my name, will teach you everything, and will call to mind all that I have told you," John 14:26, N.E.B.). The Spirit is the interpreter. An interpreter's commission is to translate ideas from one language to another, to explain hidden meanings and to introduce. A once-popular fiction character was David Grayson. In a talk with a friend, Grayson said, "Do you know what I'd like to be called? I'd like to be called an introducer. I'd like to say to my friend Mr. Blacksmith, 'Let me introduce you to my friend Mr. Plutocrat. I could almost swear you were brothers, so near alike are you. You'll find each other wonderfully interesting once you've got over the awkwardness of the introduction. . . . And Mr. White Man, let me present you particularly to my good friend Mr. Negro. You will see, if you sit down to it, that the curious color of the skin is only skin-deep.' "

3) The Spirit is the witness ("he will bear witness to me. And you also are my witnesses, because you have been with me from the first" John 15:26, 27, N.E.B.). A witness is one who says, "This is true and I know it."

Among many helpful books to consult when preaching on the Holy Spirit, one of the most lucid, readable ones is William Barclay's *The Promise of the Spirit.**

## "But you promised . . ."

TEXT: (*John 14:18, 27; 16:22; 20:19, 20*).

Introduction: What parent or grandparent has not heard the disappointed response of a child when the expectant youngster had to be told that the trip or treat or gift must be postponed? Then comes the rebuke, the verdict: "But you *promised!*" Adults soon learn that it is essential to the security and happiness of a child's life to keep promises.

Easter as a day of celebration is over for the year; but the Gospel of Easter is basic Christianity. Jesus Christ made tremendous promises to his first followers and to us. In the new *Cambridge Bible Commentary on the New English Bible,*† the professor of New Testament at the University of Aberdeen, Scotland, Dr. A. M. Hunter, has a suggestive footnote to his exposition of chapter 20 in John's Gospel. This chapter contains what the famous biblical theologian C. H. Dodd called "the most humanly moving of all the stories of the risen Christ." Here are the promises and the fulfillment: (1) "I will come back to you" (14:18). Jesus came (20:19). (2) "Peace I leave with you" (14:27). "Peace be with you" (20:19). ". . . your hearts will be filled with gladness . . ." (16:22). "The disciples were filled with joy . . ." (20:20).

Let the sermon maker take it from here. The message will not end until the hearers are told how in the seventies, busy, urban, pressured men and women can test these promises and be able to say with conviction, "I know. . . ." By practice of Christ's presence in private devotional discipline and in faithful corporate worship, by engaging in his mission in our vocation, our families, our activities as citizens, we experience the compan-

* (London: The Epworth Press, 1960).
† (Cambridge: The University Press, 1965).

ionship he promised, the peace which he alone can give, the unquenchable joy he said would be ours. "You promised, and you kept your promises."

## You can't make it alone

TEXT: "*The time is coming, and is already here, when all of you will be scattered, each one to his own home, and I will be left all alone. But I am not really alone, because the Father is with me*" (John 16:32, T.E.V.).

From time to time a glance at the gospel according to "Peanuts" is indicated. Charles Schulz, creator of the famous cartoon characters, frequently surprises us by his theological insights. A column showed Lucy playing the psychiatrist. Seated behind her little counter under the sign "Psychiatric Help, 5¢," she was dealing with Charlie Brown. Said he, "I don't know what to do . . . Sometimes I get so lonely I can hardly stand it. . . . Other times, I actually long to be completely alone . . ." Lucy gave him directive counseling: "Try to live in-between. . . . five cents, please."

1) Charlie Brown voices the plight of many men and women, boys and girls. Loneliness causes much distress. Great cities as well as small urban centers can be locations of deep loneliness. We may experience what one has called "proximity without community." In our rapidly increasing high-rise apartment complexes a person can be carried out in his coffin and the notice of his death be the first intimation his neighbors may have had that he ever lived. Jean-Paul Sartre, French existentialist, said, "Hell is other people." Sartre also said, "Without a looker-on, a man evaporates." Too many persons get "turned on" by too much alcohol, by drugs, by less harmful indulgences because they find life almost insupportable alone.

2) Why can't we make it alone where we live? Where we may visit? Because God designed life so that while solitude is essential for renewal from time to time, we cannot be whole persons until our lives are interlaced with others. Only when loneliness leads us to build good relationships with others is loneliness good. If Christ "made it alone" when his closest friends "scattered, each one to his own home," it is because he related himself vitally to God, his supreme friend. Our Lord was often alone but never lonely. As one of his followers said, "never

less alone than when alone" because the Father was with him. Christ through his Spirit enables each of us to reach the insight of Saint Joan in George Bernard Shaw's play of that name. She said to her captors and judges: ". . . my loneliness shall be my strength too: it is better to be alone with God: His friendship will not fail me, nor his counsel, nor his love. In his strength I will dare, and dare, and dare, until I die."

3) This is why the living Church is not expendable. A church deserving the name is more than an auditorium or sanctuary, important as these functions may be. It is surely more than an exclusive social club. It is a gathering of the people of God, the redemptive community, the body of Christ. Christ has given us experiences to share, tasks to do, love to know and make known to others, responsibilities to shoulder together. Too many loved and potentially lovable persons are like Willy Loman in Arthur Miller's play, *Death of a Salesman.* In his sixties Willy loses his job, is overwhelmed by despair. He can't make it alone. One night when his son takes him out for the evening, Willy's wife speaks quietly to her son: "Be kind to your father, son. He is only a little boat looking for a harbor." Christ is searching for all little lost boats. He longs to lead them into the harbor of his forgiveness, of his acceptance, of his love. You can make it alone wherever you are if with Christ's help you can say, "but I am not really alone, because the Father is with me."

## Victory then and now

TEXT: *"I have told you this so that you will have peace through your union with me. The world will make you suffer. But be brave! I have defeated the world!"* (John 16:33, T.E.V.).

Saintly Indian Bishop Azariah of Dornakal was once asked: "If you were in a village where they had never heard of Christ, what would you preach about?" He answered without hesitation: "The Resurrection." Christian preaching and witness proclaim the Lord's victory. (1) On Calvary he was mocked by enemies. After Easter he was greeted as Lord by his friends (1 Corinthians 15:11). (2) Resurrection was love's victory (John 12:32, N.E.B.). (3) Christ's resurrection is assurance that ultimate, complete victory is certain (1 Corinthians 15:24). He must conquer. He must reign.

## Stop the world, I want to get on!

TEXT: *"I sent them into the world just as you sent me into the world"* (*John 17:18, T.E.V.*).

A witty observer of the Vatican Council meetings, commenting on the impressive advances in many areas made by that ecumenical assembly, said it was proof that one of the theme songs of our Roman brothers was "Stop the world, I want to get *on!*" For centuries, loyal servants of the church were sure that the original title of the Broadway musical was more suitable: "Stop the World, I Want to Get *Off*."

Many Protestants, Orthodox, and Anglicans gave the impression that the world was something to endure, and even quietly exploit, but that it was really the devil's domain, not God's. Rediscovery of the meaning of the gospel has helped many to make a switch to the truth of John 3:16, 17: God loves this world so much he gave his only Son to save it, and this Son of his love did not come to condemn but to save the world. So we have a "holy worldliness" commanded long before Dietrich Bonhoeffer's keen insight reached us.

But to get on the world, to become involved in the world's need and sin and suffering, we must accept the directive of Christ in Matthew 28:19, 20 and reiterated in this passage from his great prayer recorded in John 17. As God sent him into the world to reclaim the world for God, so the Lord of all life sends us into the world. If we are to accomplish our mission for Christ, we must keep before us certain conditions his Spirit enables us to fulfill. We must not settle for a segment of the resources or a part of the program.

Centuries ago, the golden-mouthed preacher of the Eastern church, John Chrysostom, summarized from scripture both biblical ecumenicity (be sure to interpret this preacher's phrase for your hearers!) and the global, complete resource and goal. To get *on* the world and *in* the world to help Christ win the world I need to take (1) a whole Christ for my salvation; (2) a whole Bible for my staff; (3) a whole church for my fellowship; (4) a whole world for my parish.

[100]

## Communion in the round

TEXT: "*I do not pray only for them, but also for those who believe in me because of their message. I pray that they may all be one. O Father! May they be in us, just as you are in me and I am in you. May they be one, so that the world will believe that you sent me*" (*John 17:20, 21, T.E.V.*).

Churches in the round are familiar since architecture joined with liturgical revival in both Protestant and Roman churches.

1) Worship "in the round," even in traditional types of buildings, increases the sense of community. Physical proximity does not of itself insure spiritual intimacy, although it may help. Said the Texan to the "foreigner" who asked if Texas was so large that the earth's population could be contained in it: "Yes sir, if they were all friends!" However aesthetically satisfying the altar type of communion table may be, Christian theologians increasingly urge that the "holy table" be as close to the people as possible. Christ is the host and it is *his* table, and we who join him in this strange and wonderful Supper are his friends.

2) Communion in the round (as on World-Wide Communion Sunday) should symbolize the truth that the world is God's area of operations and therefore in a deep, ecumenical sense our parish. British biblical scholar William Neil asserts that chapters 14–17 of John's Gospel bring us nearer Christ's mind than any other chapters. Great themes are in them as well as great words. Peace, love, and unity are the themes. All three—and not least, unity—should be experienced in the Lord's Supper. John 17:20 reaches out to embrace all who through apostolic preaching commit themselves to Christ. Verse 21 answers the question how Christians achieve unity. As in the relationship between Father and Son, so in the personal relationship of mutual love. It is the "I–Thou" relationship made famous by the late Professor Martin Buber. Our demonstrated unity will be the convincing argument to the world that Christ is God's embodiment and that God's love is real and invincible.

3) Communion in the round must celebrate and demonstrate the Good News of John 3:16, 17. God loves not just the white, Gentile, Christian, church-supporting world, but

the whole world of persons. "Whosoever will may come" and must be sought and welcomed and at last by divine grace incorporated into the mystical body of Christ, the community of believers redeemed and redeeming. As the first Duke of Wellington said 150 years ago, when a former subordinate army veteran asked parish church communicants to make way for "His Grace, the Duke of Wellington": "No, no! we are all alike here." Enter communion in the round without rank, prejudice, pride, despair.

## What was finished at Calvary?

TEXT: *"It is finished!"* (*John 19:30, T.E.V.*).

As we prepare to lead our people with ourselves into a meaningful, creative Lenten experience, this question may be asked and answered: "What was finished at Calvary?" Many bystanders then and many since have been sure that Christ's own life was certainly ended, finished; that his dream of God's fatherly rule over all mankind was given a death blow. New Testament scholar Archibald M. Hunter of Aberdeen, Scotland, once answered this question by quoting three picture phrases from Jesus' own words. In these Dr. Hunter is sure we have the answer to the question. (1) "Christ saw his passion and death as a cup to be drunk" (Matthew 26:39). (2) "Christ saw his passion as a road to be traveled" (Mark 14:21). (3) "Christ saw his passion as a price to be paid" (Matthew 20:28). He drank the cup to the dregs. He traveled the road to the end and beyond. He paid the price redemptive love must pay. Over them all could be written, "Finished!" "Completed"—in full.

## Man alive!

TEXT: (*John 20:19–21, T.E.V.*).

Who doesn't remember singing the children's hymn in which the wistful refrain occurs, "I wish I had been with him then"? To many who profess the Christian faith, Christ is still the Jesus of history, not the Christ of present experience. When they read of highly intellectual, carefully trained scholars speaking of Christ as "the eternal contemporary" it sounds as if the phrase was only a kind of poetry, not necessarily descriptive of something real. Nevertheless, nineteen centuries of Christian experience make it clear that, like the first Christians after Christ's resurrection, for many in every generation since, Christians did not *remember* Jesus, but *experienced* him as a living Lord and present companion and helper. Again and again, persons of different temperament, many of them not the "mystical type," spoke of his living presence. Think of the missionary explorer of the last century, David Livingstone, telling Cambridge University students that what sustained him in Africa was the presence of a Gentleman who promised, "Lo, I am with you alway . . ."

How can we know Christ as "man alive"—a living presence?

1) We need to remind ourselves that if Christ was raised from the dead, he is alive today; and if alive, then our contemporary; and if our contemporary, we may "meet" him, even if we do not have physical, visible, or audible encounter with him.

2) In the early church, as the New Testament makes clear, the living Lord was generally known to be alive and in and among his own when his followers met together in fellowship. He had said in one of the most profound statements ever made concerning the social worship of God: "For where two or three come together in my name, I am there with them" (Matthew 18:20). Professor William Barclay of Glasgow University rightly pointed out that Thomas missed seeing the risen Jesus because he was absent from the fellowship of the ten disciples. When we isolate ourselves from the church at worship and at work and play, may we not be isolating ourselves from Christ?

3) Christ comes to us in unmistakable power when we are proceeding on the kind of task he would wish us to undertake in our community and world. Said a twentieth-century disciple, "Christ gives himself to those who give themselves to him in commitment and effort." When we love him, he draws near; when we are in the worshiping company of others who have made him Lord and Master, when we are men and women for others as he is the man for others, he makes himself known to us as alive. The little girl made an inspired misquotation when she said that the Lord Jesus promised, "*Glow*, I am with you always, even to the end of the world." Life glows with his presence when we experience his companionship.

## Resurrection reassurances

TEXT: (*John 20:19–31; 1 Corinthians 15:17; Luke 7:1–17; 8:40–56; 16:19–31, T.E.V.*).

These passages provide a possible fourfold treatment of the theme. Each of them gives an example of the risen Lord's power to raise people from the dead. Much better use of these passages and themes would be in a series for the four Sundays after Easter.

1) Faith is "for real." In 1 Corinthians 15:17 (R.S.V.) the statement is blunt: "If Christ has not been raised, your faith is futile . . ." Jesus did not criticize Thomas' request that he have firsthand evidence of the resurrection. "If I do not see . . . I will not believe" (John 20:25). Why do we know our faith in the living Lord is not futile? Because we too have experienced the risen Christ.

2) God gives life. When the Roman officer had his interview with Jesus, the Roman recognized that Jesus operates with God's power. "Just give the order and my servant will get well" (Luke 7:7). Similarly, the restoration of the widow's son to life caused the crowd to attribute the action to God: "God has come to save his people!" (verse 16). To the Christian has been given life-giving power, through the Christian's obedience and trust (John 14:12).

3) Hope conquers fear. It is the hope of life which destroys the fear of death. Consider how the quaking disciples, huddled together behind locked doors for fear, had their fear replaced by the appearance of the risen Christ (John 20:19–20). Where Christ comes there is peace; where he is accepted there is healing; where he is obeyed there is invincible courage.

4) How skeptical can we get? "But Abraham said, "If they will not listen to Moses and the prophets, they will not be convinced even if someone were to rise from death' " (Luke 16:31). Just as music and visual arts leave some people unmoved and unwon, so there are persons to whom the resurrection of Christ conveys no idea of God's power. Skepticism can be held stubbornly and often to "protect" the skeptic from the commitment and other consequences of belief. Not a few today discount God's activity completely. "Who needs God?" they ask—if not in words then in their attitudes and actions. This message should, in the words of one of Dr. Harry Emerson

Fosdick's sermons, encourage skeptics to "doubt their doubts." A once famous University of Chicago president, the late Dr. William Rainey Harper, said to students: "Why didn't someone tell me that I can become a Christian and settle the doubts afterwards?"

## Absent without leave

TEXT: "*One of the disciples, Thomas (called the Twin), was not with them when Jesus came*" (*John 20:24, T.E.V.*).

1) He should have been. He missed so much, being "absent without leave" from the fellowship of Christ's men. Doubtless Thomas felt it was futile to meet for prayer and togetherness and directions now that the Commander was gone, as Thomas thought, never to return. He could rejoin them later when his deep sense of bereavement and disappointment and despair had passed. On the Sunday following Easter Day many of the Lord's present-day men and women are A.W.O.L., as soldiers would say. After all, they had shown their loyalty by being in the Upper Room, at church on the great day. This is not why the first Sunday after Easter was designated Low Sunday in the church calender, but it often is low in attendance, vitality, and creative fellowship.

2) Thomas should have been present when Jesus came, even if he doubted that Jesus ever would come. First, because Thomas needed more than memory; he needed *meeting*. "Real life is meeting," said World Council of Churches pioneer J. H. Oldham. We need each other if the inner loneliness is to be banished and a sense of the greatness of the Christian enterprise in the world is to be sustained. We need meeting in worship that we may discharge "our bounden duty" to God and offer our best in adoring love and take from him his grace for daily living. Thomas should have been there to meet his risen Lord. It would have resolved his doubts at least eight days earlier. This is why public worship of God is indispensable to healthy spiritual life.

3) Thomas should have been with the others in the Upper Room, bringing his unbelief and broken hopes to experience the *miracle* of the living Lord. Said an old country gardener about the Isle of Iona and its ancient Christian association,

"The veil is very thin there." In church at worship, the veil is very thin between the seeker of reality in Christ and the unseen, living Lord. He keeps his promise: "For wherever two or three people come together in my name [in my spirit, in my faith, drawn together as my followers], I am there, right among them!" (Matthew 18:20, J.B.P.).

4) Thomas should have been there with the other followers of Jesus to receive the *mission.* Said the risen Christ after his blessing of peace: "As the Father has sent me, even so I send you" (John 20:21, R.S.V.). To extend the church's ministry into the world we need not only the truth of "religionless (or secularized) Christianity," but renewal of our life in the mystery of worship, in the companionship of the living Lord. First worship, then work. First the contact with God, then the commission. First the meeting and the miracle, then the mission. Thomas did not stay away. "Eight days later, his disciples were again in the house, and Thomas was with them. The doors were shut, but Jesus came and stood among them, . . ." (John 20:26, R.S.V.). Thomas and Martha, don't stay away too long. Join us in the renewal and reinforcement that always comes when we meet with Christ and one another.

## Realizing the presence

TEXT: "*. . . he showed himself to them many times, in ways that proved beyond doubt that he was alive; . . .*" (*Acts 1:3,* T.E.V.).

To use an idiom with which at least teen-agers are familiar we might say, "Is Christ for real, man?" Christians of every age and temperament would concede that much in Christianity may be duplicated in other religions and philosophies and codes of ethics. But Jesus is unique. He remains God's new power which makes all the difference. But except for rare mystical moments which some of the more prosaic of us may never experience, he seems a fact of history rather than the warm, sweet, tender person depicted in some sentimental hymns.

How can men and women experience Christ's living presence without going psychic or "spooky"? For the church on the main line of its witness claims that Jesus Christ is alive.

True, the living Lord and the Holy Spirit seem interchangeable names for the same reality in both the New Testament and the testimonies of Christians. Christ is our eternal contemporary. For the church is the community of the resurrection. The central belief of this community is that Christ who was put to death was raised from the dead, and if raised from the dead, alive and knowable. A famous Scottish theologian, James Denney, said, "No apostle ever *remembered* Jesus." They did not remember him because he was not dead but alive, in and with and among his own.

If we take the experience of the young church as reflected and described in the book of the Acts of the Apostles, facts or clues emerge.

1) He appears to us, to the eyes of faith, if we love him. Not to Caiaphas or Annas or Pilate, but to Mary of Magdala and the others who loved him did Christ make himself known after his death. From the Apostle Paul to St. Francis of Assisi to David Livingstone to Albert Schweitzer to Martin Luther King, and to the humblest and most obscure Christian, Christ has shown himself alive, because each loved him and tried to obey him in daily life.

2) Generally speaking, is it not true also that the loving Christ manifests himself to his followers when they are in fellowship together. We have his promise and he is a gentleman who keeps his word (Matthew 18:20). The Apostle Thomas missed him on that memorable evening in the Upper Room because "he was not with them." Do you want to find the risen and living Lord? Join some of his friends in worship, in planning, in study, in friendship.

3) Proceed on some part of Christ's program. Engage in work Christ inspires and must want carried to successful conclusion. See Acts 18:1 and Acts 23:11. As Professor William Barclay expressed it, "Jesus gives himself to those who give themselves to him in commitment and effort." There is no place where Christ is not—when we become involved in Christian social action. He is "where the action is."

## "All signals are 'Go!' "

TEXT: "*And when they came together, he gave them this order: 'Do not leave Jerusalem, but wait for the gift my Father promised, that I told you about. For John baptized with water, but in a few days you will be baptized with the Holy Spirit.'"* (*Acts 1:4, 5, T.E.V.*).

Few of us are so blasé that we are not excited by the exploits of the astronauts. "Walking on air" is now not just a figure of speech to express ecstasy. Many spacecraft phrases are familiar: "A-O.K." and "All systems are 'Go!'"

2) This means the extension of the church's ministry into the world as we know it at our doors, where we work or study or teach or play, and also in those depressed and impoverished communities which we often tire of hearing about—the inner city and the slums, urban and rural. Harvey Cox's stimulating, disturbing study *The Secular City** surveys and analyzes the "theater" of the Christian church's "warfare."

3) When all signals in our contemporary society say "Go!" the signals are not for the elite spacecraft team—in the church's mission this means the clergy or full-time religious workers—the signals are for all Christians, for the ministry of the laity and the laity of the ministry are gospel facts.

When Edward Lindaman of the moon-shot program roused commissioners at a May 1965 assembly of churchmen, it was because he rang the changes on "Go!" rather than "Come!" His proposal was heartily endorsed, but only after one amendment. What was the amendment? That we would first obey our Lord's command in Acts 1:4, that we wait and listen for the Spirit's leading and then obey him. They were to wait, not in a lovely retreat center by seashore, lake or on mountain summit, but in the same teeming, troublesome, and often ugly city. To advance, Christians must first abide. See John 15:4, 5. No astronaut could have walked outside his spacecraft a hundred miles above the planet if the lifeline to his "ship" had been severed. "Without me," said Christ, "you can do nothing." We are worthless and impotent when we are detached from him. Wait, then obey the signals. He gives power for the mission he assigns to us.

## Time and seasons

TEXT: "*Jesus said to them: 'The times and occasions are set by my Father's own authority, and it is not for you to*

* (New York: The Macmillan Company, 1965).

*know when they will be'* " (*Acts 1:7, T.E.V.*). "*There is no need to write you, brothers, about the times and occasions when these things will happen*" (*1 Thessalonians 5:1*).

1) No genuine reason exists for beginning the New Year on January first. Jews, Moslems, schools, and universities do not keep our calendar. But without some stable arrangement of time, ordered life would be impossible. However, we need to realize that chronological division of time is inadequate to provide a true setting for our lives. This is where the New Testament comes to help.

2) "Times and seasons" is a phrase which is used in Acts at the time of the Ascension of Christ and also in Thessalonians by Paul when he informed his fellow disciples that they had no need to know fixed dates for the Day of the Lord. Thanks to scholars such as Professor Oscar Cullman, we understand more clearly that two words are used, and different words. "Time" comes from the Greek word *chronos*, having to do with the chronological (think of our word chronometer), and *kairos* for season, which is independent of clocks, watches, calendars. "Time" is scriptural recognition of the normal way we count time. "Season," for which *kairos* is used, means the right time, the time of decision, of opportunity, of judgment (see Matthew 16:3; Luke 19:44; Mark 13:32, 33; Colossians 4:5; Ephesians 5:17).

3) Christians live in a "season," God-given, independent of ordinary time. So at this annual division of calendar time we need to face the challenge of Romans 13:11 and 2 Corinthians 6:2. It is high time to wake up to reality. "Now, I say, has the hour of deliverance dawned."

## "Both . . . and"

TEXT: "*But you will be filled with power when the Holy Spirit comes on you, and you will be witnesses for me in Jerusalem, in all of Judea and Samaria, and to the ends of the earth*" (*Acts 1:8, T.E.V.*).

1) Here is the answer to a pressing question among Christians in our time. The question is this: Where can Christian witness and work best be done? Some argue that the institutional church is moribund, irrelevant, inept—a kind of religious ghetto isolated from the mainstream of life. Others

argue that unconventional or special ministries are a delusion and a snare for the men and women who find "a local habitation and a name" repulsive. The answer is given in the commission handed Christ's first followers of the Risen Lord. It is not either the storefront church, the coffeehouse "happening," the house-church, or the chapel, church, or cathedral. It is "both . . . and." Once we realize that we are to be Christ's witnesses ("you will be witnesses for me"), then it is evident that Christ wants us to witness to him and to his gospel where we are and then on into all the world.

2) This means that we have a center and a headquarters —where we are—in the local congregation. Granted, many members are in the preschool stage of the Christian life; many are petty, puerile, and rigid in their adherence to the old and obsolete. But always there is the saving remnant, those whom Jesus called the salt of the earth and the light of the world. Moreover, the church in its local expression provides a base, supplies for the campaign in the world outside and recruits for the active service force. ". . . you will be witnesses for me," said Christ, "in Jerusalem. . . ." Right where we are, we are to be witnesses. This means for most Christians the church on Main Street, downtown, or in suburbia. Nothing is true until it becomes local.

3) Our witness and fellowship, our work to Christianize persons, institutions, politics, economic life, is not to be limited to our parish, to our neighborhood, our town or city. "You will be witnesses for me in Jerusalem, in all Judea and Samaria, and to the ends of the earth." Christianity circumscribed by geographical or social or any other boundaries is a Christianity sorely limited and distorted.

Do we want to keep something infinitely good that we have experienced for ourselves and our kind alone? If we do, we shall lose the "unspeakable (unsurpassed) riches" we have in Christ. As a Christian businessman said in answer to a fellow official in a local church who objected to world mission giving: "If our religion isn't good enough for the export business, it isn't good enough for home consumption." Could our apparent ineffectiveness be due to our neglect of one or the other? "Isn't there enough to do here at home?" is the perennial objection of the parochially minded. Of course, there is plenty to do at home, and we must never stop doing it. But it can never be "either/or." Our Lord insisted that it must be "both/and."

## Why the Resurrection?

TEXT: "*The God of our fathers raised Jesus from death, after you had killed him by nailing him to a cross*" (*Acts 5:30, T.E.V.*).

A generation that questions everything may well ask, "But why the Resurrection? Why become excited about the return of your noble teacher from death? Isn't it enough that you have his teachings, his example, his ethic?" Peter—and the other apostles—gave a basic reason when he said to the angry high priest, "And God raised him to his right side as Leader and Savior, to give to the people of Israel the opportunity to repent and have their sins forgiven" (Acts 5:31). We would add, "and to all who by trusting faith are truly in the new Israel, the people of God." Consider these further reasons for the Resurrection. God's purpose in raising Jesus from the dead, not merely resuscitating his dead physical body, was (a) to give God's "Yes" to the world's "No." Good Friday convinced the "world" that Jesus was wrong, deluded, the victim of an impossible faith. Easter reversed the verdict. (b) Christ's Resurrection rebuilt the shattered faith of Christ's first followers. The church was created, partly at least, because the disciples were recreated by their experience of the living Lord whom death could not destroy. "We are witnesses to these things— . . ." (verse 32). No living Lord, no living church; it is as simple and as real as that. (c) To give us hope that the world itself will be recreated, reconstituted. Christianity, said a contemporary Anglican bishop, Mervyn Stockwood, "is not a recipe for personal salvation but a way of cosmic redemption." See and quote Romans 8:18–21 in either the New English Bible or the J. B. Phillips translation.

## What to preach

TEXT: "*Philip went to the city of Samaria and preached the Messiah to the people there*" (*Acts 8:5, T.E.V.*).

What to preach? This is a question which has plagued more than one responsible preacher. Of course the true answer for the Christian, whether a full-time minister or a minister who might call himself a layman, is: "Preach Christ."

Said John Wesley of his own service of Christ: "I offered them Christ." To proclaim Christ is the commission given every Christian, whether he is a church's pastor or a man or woman in any occupation. We are to be his witnesses. But preaching Christ may be what the late beloved Hal Luccock called "swinging the Protestant incense," that is, indulging in glittering, even pious generalities. We need to spell out what the great phrase means.

In a "charge to the minister" (which is wise counsel and not anything in the nature of electrical energizing), a remarkable veteran of the preaching and pastoral ministry, Samuel Macaulay Lindsay, spelled out preaching Christ for a grateful younger brother being inducted into his new pastorate.

You may need to transmit this word to your own fellow preachers—proclaimers—members of your congregation. You may find "starters" for a "charge" you may give to a brother or sister assuming a pastorate.

"Remember (1) you are expected to clarify and amplify our conception of God. (2) You are expected to announce that the Christ way is the best way for the New Day. (3) You are expected to awaken within each of us the desire to be a Christ in miniature. (4) You are expected to proclaim that the best days of humanity are ahead of us and not behind us." (God cannot be defeated. His kingdom must come, either within or beyond history.) "I charge you," continued the prophet, Dr. Lindsay, "to proclaim your faith in God. He awakens; he enriches; he empowers. Have faith in Christ. He heals; he instructs; he redeems. Have faith in man. At his Christian best, man believes in God, in doing what is right, in life eternal through Christ."

## Know any encouragers?

TEXT: "*The news about this reached the church in Jerusalem, so they sent Barnabas to Antioch. When he arrived and saw how God had blessed the people, he was glad and urged them all to be faithful and true to the Lord with all their hearts. Barnabas was a good man, full of the Holy*

[112] **Know any encouragers?**

*Spirit and faith. Many people were brought to the Lord"* (*Acts 11:22–24*).

You know some discouragers, the so-called "realists" who take a dim view of almost everything. In every parish there is the lugubrious saint who says, "It's a good idea, but I'd like to know where we can get the money." In his or her eyes is that "It's hopeless" look.

Here was a Cypriot farmer who liquidated his assets to become a Christian worker. He was rightly named Barnabas; the name means "encourager." God's hand was in their choice of this encourager to handle the Antioch situation. He had proven his love, his loyalty, his generosity (see Acts 9:27; 15:25, 26, 37). Every significant enterprise, every congregation, needs a Barnabas, and more than one if advance is to be made. The true encourager is himself a man of goodness, obviously inspired by God's Spirit and equipped with an intelligent, robust faith (Acts 11:24).

1) Blessed are the reconcilers, for they shall help different and differing types to live and work together for God's cause. The church must demonstrate that it is dynamically a beloved community. One reconciling person can work wonders. So a New Testament scholar has called Barnabas "the biggest heart in the church."

2) Encouragers are effective evangelists. In Acts 11:24 we read, "Many people were brought to the Lord." Barnabas cared about persons. A Christian church is a caring church. A caring church is a growing church.

3) Encouragers within the Christian community are courageous people. Read Acts 13:2 to see that Barnabas and Saul had to be brave to tackle the kind of people they did. Barnabas, like all encouragers, could play on the team: he was a colleague and partner of Paul. He did not think of being a Christian leader on his "wild lone." Encouragers help the church to coordinate its work. "Only the whole church can preach the whole gospel to the whole world." Is it any wonder that in Antioch the Christians were first called Christians? What was at first a half-mocking nickname became a world-renowned name. When Christians love, care, show courage, and encourage others to do their best, the world watches, wonders, and admires.

## He's given you some clues

TEXT: *"But he has always given proof of himself by the good things he does: he gives you rain from heaven and crops at the right times; he gives you food and fills your hearts with happiness"* (Acts 14:17, T.E.V.).

To superstitious "backwoods" folk of Asia Minor in the first century of our era, the Apostle Paul spoke these words. His hearers mistook the early Christian missionaries for gods in disguise. Paul and Barnabas protested and, after affirming their own humanity ("We are only human beings, no less mortal than you"), they urged the people to believe the good news they brought and "to turn to the living God," the Creator of all. Today the church proclaims the same good news, through evangelists urges our contemporaries to turn to the living God. Whether or not the residents of ancient Lystra responded so, many of us and of our fellow citizens could say, "But can we know God?" Few are militant atheists. We may not even be among the radical theologians who sadly announce that God is dead. Most of us feel that there must be a Mind other than human at work in this mysterious universe; it seems highly unlikely that it organized itself. But we would like to have more than opinions about a possible deity. Is it because we are not among those who have a highly developed mystical sense? Moreover, reason alone seems incapable of discovering God. We understand that Christianity claims that the way to God is open to all, however simple or however intellectual they may be. How can we know God?

Every pastor knows that in his congregation are some who could speak in such terms. There are sincere agnostics who deeply desire to believe in God. To such unconvinced, honest seekers we may say as did Paul: God "has not left you without some clue to his nature." Every normal human being has the capacity to know God, not just the gifted mystic, the saint, the person who accepts without question the authority of a so-called infallible church.

1) *"Look around you,"* said the famous woman saint, Theresa, to her pupils when they asked her for evidence of God's reality. Look at the action of the loving God in the order and design and providential provisions of this mysterious

universe, Paul appears to have said to the Lystra citizens. Nowhere does the Bible try to prove God's existence, but the Bible does not pooh-pooh away what is at least a partial revelation of God in the universe around us (see Romans 1:20).

2) There is a clue to God's reality and activity in what is called the *moral* law (Romans 2:14, N.E.B.). It may not be "saving knowledge" but it is knowledge.

3) Again, God gives us a clue in what he has done and is doing in *history*. Amos 9:7 is worth thinking about, and its insight worth applying to other nations than Israel and other eras than that of Amos. Granted that all these are partial clues and, as our soundest theologians remind us, partial knowledge distorted by human sinfulness.

4) The master clue God gives us is through the history of ancient Israel fulfilled and completed in what is rightly called the *Christ Event:* the personality, teaching, sacrificial death, resurrection, and continued life within the Christian community of Jesus Christ.

5) With these clues we must act. Faith and obedience are inseparable. God is most surely known when we confide ourselves to him, doubts and all, and proceed to do what we believe he desires us to do within the community of faith and service. "If any man will do his will, he shall know. . . ." After all, what are the doubts of persons like ourselves compared to the faith of Jesus Christ?

## Religious troublemakers

TEXT: "*They brought them* [*Paul and Silas*] *before the Roman officials and said: 'These men are . . . causing trouble in our city'* " (*Acts 16:20, T.E.V.*).

1) Christianity, authentic and apostolic, always causes trouble for those who may suffer financial or other kinds of loss through a more Christian way of life. Look at the incident in this chapter. An emotionally disturbed girl had proved a source of income for her owners as a professional fortune teller. She found in Paul's message and concern that which enabled the Spirit of God to heal her. Thereafter she was no longer a money-maker. So her owners grabbed the apostles and

charged them with being a public nuisance and causing trouble in the city.

2) Christians are not called to be troublemakers just for the sake of upsetting the "establishment," but they are to emulate the first disciples who turned an upside-down society right side up.

3) All through history Christians have caused trouble in cities—from Nazareth and Capernaum and Jerusalem to Athens, to London and Birmingham, to Montgomery and Washington. Not all the trouble in such cities was caused by Christians; invariably more violent and militant characters exploited the situation.

4) If Christ and his cause does not upset us in the city of Mansoul (to use a quaint word from John Bunyan), we have a right to question its validity. Writes John B. Nettleship in *British Weekly*, ". . . with all the necessary emphasis on the comfort that our Christian faith can bring, we must not forget this stern aspect. Light and salt, which were used by Jesus to illustrate the quality of Christian discipleship, have healing, cleansing power. But it is perhaps worth remembering that light can dazzle and annoy, that salt can make a wound smart. The very process of healing and cleansing can sometimes be a painful one."

## Notes of the resurrection trumpet

TEXT: (*Acts 17:16–34, T.E.V.*).

A great Scottish preacher, describing the Apostle Paul's experience as a Christian preacher in sophisticated, speculative Athens, pictured him ending his religious generalities and putting "the Resurrection trumpet to his lips." "Men of Athens," he declares, "I am here to tell you that God has broken through into history. God has raised up Christ and by this deed has changed the whole human situation and the universe itself radically and decisively. He has vindicated righteousness and defeated the dark powers forever!" *

The trumpet notes sounded are: (1) Christ is Lord of

* James S. Stewart, A *Faith to Proclaim*, pp. 113, 114.

life and death (Philippians 2:9–11). (2) Justice, God's righteousness is vindicated. As one has written, "The Resurrection is not just a personal survival: it is a cosmic victory" (See T. S. Eliot's play, *Murder in the Cathedral* at the opening of the cathedral doors).* (3) We can share Christ's risen life here and now (Ephesians 1:19, 20). The energy which took Christ out of the tomb is available to help us live and to do the things Christ wants us to do (see 2 Corinthians 5:17). (4) We are companions of the living Lord on every road we take (Romans 6:5). (5) We share Christ's life in the redeemed and redeeming community, the church. (6) The final note sounds the defeat of death.

## What to do when all seems lost

TEXT: "*They were afraid that our ship would go on the rocks, so they lowered four anchors from the back of the ship and prayed for daylight*" (*Acts 27:29, T.E.V.*).

Following Christ and trusting him should make a person of average intelligence superior to the non-Christian in a crisis. Christianity began in a crisis, a crucial one for its future: the crucifixion of the founder and master. Repeatedly in history the Christian church has experienced severe storm and stress. In one of the finest and most dramatic narratives of a storm at sea the Apostle Paul gives a demonstration of how to behave as Christians when all seems lost. The late Henry Sloane Coffin, a superb sermon maker, outlined what Paul provided by way of spiritual anchors: (1) He kept everyone on board; there were no crippling desertions. (2) He kept up their normal life (". . . Paul begged them all to eat some food . . ."—verse 33). (3) He had the grace of gratitude (". . . Paul took some bread, gave thanks to God before them all . . ."—verse 35). (4) He infected his fellow voyagers with his contagious faith ("They took courage . . ."—verse 36).

Another possible pattern for this verse about anchors is James S. Stewart's: The first anchor is hope. The second is duty. The third is prayer. The fourth is the Cross of Christ.

A lesser known preacher (Arthur E. Dalton of St. Law-

* (New York: Harcourt, Brace & World, Inc., 1935, 1963).

rence, Jersey, in the Channel Islands) chose this pattern: (1) The Anchor of Common Sense. (2) The Anchor of Christian Conviction. (3) The Anchor of Christian Patience. (4) The Anchor of Christian Courage.

## Saints without God?

TEXT: "*And so I write to all of you in Rome whom God loves and has called to be his own people . . .*" (*Romans 1:7*, T.E.V.). "*Then Jacob awoke from his sleep and said, 'Surely the Lord is in this place; and I did not know it'* " (*Genesis 28:16*, R.S.V.).

November 1 in the Christian calendar is All Saints' Day. Even the most convinced nonconformist Protestants have something of a tender attitude toward this ancient festival. As the *Book of Common Order* of the United Church describes it, "At this time we remember the faithful in Christ who have finished their course on earth; and we pray, that encouraged by their examples and strengthened by their fellowship, we also may be found meet to be partakers of the inheritance of the saints in light." In New Testament usage a saint is a Christian, a person who has responded to Christ's call and self-giving by commitment to Christ and obedience to his Spirit. So J. B. Phillips translates Romans 1:7: "To you all then, loved of God and called to be Christ's men and women. . . ." N.E.B. renders the phrase: "all . . . whom God loves and has called to be his dedicated people."

1) What of the "saints" who demonstrate qualities of saintliness and yet who would hesitate to say that they are believers in God and disciples of Christ? A famous French writer, the late Albert Camus, wrote as an avowed humanist. Nevertheless, students of his own life as a resistance fighter in World War II and of his writings find in him authentic if "unchurchly" saintliness. In his book *The Plague** he has a character say, "My problem is how to be a saint without God." Camus apparently considered this to be also the problem of many men and women in this modern era. Camus, in his own personality and in the best of his novels' characters, exhibited the concern for

* (New York: Alfred A. Knopf, Inc., 1948).

the oppressed and suffering, the caring for others, the championship of true justice and compassion, which are surely marks of the "saints," of the "loved of God . . . called to be Christ's men and women."

2) To be truly human is to be Christian. To be truly Christian and human is not easy without God. As William Martin wrote: "Perhaps it is not so easy to be man without God. Perhaps in seeking to be a saint without God, man is straining the limits of his own nature, and deliberately ignoring the only conditions under which he may successfully become a genuine human being." * What if the avowed humanists are aided and abetted by the great God whose reality they deny or ignore? What if, as to Cyprus of old, God could say to such moral heroes and spiritual leaders, "I girded thee though thou hast not known me" (Isaiah 45:5, K.J.V.)? George Macdonald (1824–1905) has a wonderful poem, "The Presence of Christ," about the living Christ being present and active in any life which turned away from "ill" and turned toward the high and heroic, asked for forgiveness, and went out into a grim world with hope.

3) Like Jacob after his dream, we need to awaken to the presence and power of the One who may come to us "all unknown" but who is within this tangled human situation. He does strengthen us within by his Spirit and has the final word in the war between good and evil. He finds us through the community of Christ we call the church. One day we too may say, "Surely the Lord is in this place, this experience, this person, this company of Christians, and I did not know it until now."

## The peril, the promise, and the power

TEXT: *"God's wrath is revealed coming down from heaven upon all the sin and evil of men, whose evil ways prevent the truth from being known."* (*Romans 1:18*, T.E.V.)

On October 2, 1968, a Christian leader died. He was editor of an influential ecumenical weekly journal, *The Christian Century*, and also editor of a minister's magazine, *The Pulpit.* His name was Kyle Haselden. He was deeply concerned about the kind of preaching all of us who occupy pulpits

* *British Weekly*, June 29, 1967, p. 6.

do. In his book, *The Urgency of Preaching,* Dr. Haselden expressed his conviction that Christian preaching would be rescued from mediocrity and banality when we "restore in ourselves an urgent sense of the human Peril, confidence in the divine Promise, and trust in God's Power to transform the one into the other." * Look at this "divine triangle."

1) Effective Christian preaching always sounds the note of warning. When you and I warn someone we give notice that a danger or an evil is near. We are not threatening. So often when we come to church we hear no warnings but something more nearly resembling lullabies. "Peace, perfect peace" is the favorite theme if not the favorite hymn of many excellent people. The pastor as preacher does not try to "scare the daylights" out of his friends in the pews. However, through the scriptures, warning is sounded as in our first scripture. What about the threat of atomic war, of racial violence, of widespread hunger, of the moral decay and social decadence not of the "new morality," but of the old immorality? The Bible warns us of "the dire consequences which alienation from God and disobedience to his will have upon *this* life." † This alienation shows itself in society in wars, racial conflict, ghettos, political crookedness, and much else. In individual persons it shows itself in what the Germans call *angst* and we call anxiety, morbid fears, bitterness, hollow lives, depression.

The church must help us all face the Peril, and then confront (2) the Promise. Just before Peter spoke of the promise in his famous Jerusalem sermon the apostle was asked, "Brethren, what shall we do?" (Acts 2:37, R.S.V.). He answered: "Repent, and be baptized every one of you in the name of Jesus Christ for the forgiveness of your sins; and you shall receive the gift of the Holy Spirit. For the promise is to you . . . " (Acts 2:38–39, R.S.V.). Never must we send you away from church utterly depressed. Grave is the peril, genuine is the warning, but gloriously true is the divine promise of forgiveness, acceptance, newness of life and (3) Empowerment. For God's Yes is always set over against his No (see the text 2 Corinthians 1:19–20 and also Luke 12:31).

In the biblical drama of salvation, what Dr. Haselden called "the active agent, the determinative Alterant" is the

* (New York: Harper & Row, Publishers, 1963), p. 42.
† *Ibid.*, p. 45.

God who makes himself known redemptively in the "man for others," Jesus Christ. You wonder how we can escape the horrors of a world and of a life separated from God and seemingly headed for colossal disaster? You wonder how the blessings of the Promise can be obtained? Behold the man who is also God-in-a-human-life, Jesus Christ. In him "all the promises of God find their Yes." A brilliant Hindu intellectual is quoted as saying, perhaps derisively, "Christians are an ordinary people who make extraordinary claims." This is gloriously true. We are unmistakably ordinary, but we have extraordinary claims to make "that Jesus Christ is the incomparable, irreplaceable, indispensable Alterant between the world's Peril and God's Promise." *

## "O love of God! O sin of man!"

TEXT: ". . . *all men have sinned and are far away from God's saving presence*" (*Romans 3:23, T.E.V.*).

"*But God's mercy is so abundant, and his love for us is so great, that while we were spiritually dead in our disobedi ence he brought us to life with Christ; it is by God's grace that you have been saved. In our union with Christ Jesus he raised us up with him to rule with him in the heavenly world. He did this to demonstrate for all time to come the abundant riches of his grace in the love he showed us in Christ Jesus*" (*Ephesians 2:4–7*).

From the hymn by the late Frederick W. Faber, "O Come and Mourn with Me Awhile," come the words of our theme, "O love of God! O sin of man!" True, we do not stress the reality of sin and the necessity of conversion in ways dear to Faber and his nineteenth-century fellow Christians. Nevertheless, in the Cross of Christ we see both the love of God and the sin of man clearly and starkly. Until we do see them we cannot understand our predicament and that of all human beings, nor can we understand the meaning of Christ's death.

1) The New Testament makes the most searching analysis of man's "fallenness." "All men have sinned"—including the Christian and the non-Christian, the respectable and the "scum" of society (see Romans 7:14, 18, 19, 24). This is no

* *Ibid.*, p. 69.

morbid preoccupation with the seamy side of human nature and behavior. Sin, the New Testament makes clear, is alienation from God, hostility to him, rebellion against him and his design for his human family. This is placarded before us in the crucifixion of Jesus Christ (1 Corinthians 2:8). Sin is evident everywhere, but it is disclosed at its worst at Golgotha. (Acts 3:13–15; 5:30; 10:36–39 show how earliest Christian preaching included this fact.) Yet this is not the whole story, thank God.

2) In the Cross is demonstrated God's love. ". . . while we were still sinners . . . Christ died for us!" (Romans 5:8). Here the second text, Ephesians 2:4–7, declares the same tremendous, transforming truth and power. God's love and Christ's love are interchangeable terms (see John 3:16 and Galatians 2:20). "This is what love is" wrote the prophet John, ". . . not that we loved God, but that he loved us and sent his Son . . ." (1 John 4:10). ". . . we know what love is: Christ gave his life for us. We too, then, ought to give our lives for our brothers!" (1 John 3:16).

3) God's victory is sure. As the hymn expresses it:

*O love of God! O sin of man!*
*In this dread act your strength is tried;*
*And victory remains with love;*
*For thou, our Lord, art crucified!*
*F. W. Faber, 1814–1863*

Yes, crucified and risen. Resurrection confirms the victory (see Romans 8:32–34; Colossians 2:9–15).

## The Cross: God's own proof of his love

TEXT: *"But God has shown us how much he loves us: it was while we were still sinners that Christ died for us!" (Romans 5:8, T.E.V.).*

1) To create was easy; to convert was costly. The late Archbishop of Canterbury, William Temple, spoke to a university audience on the meaning of the Cross. He began by quoting two scripture passages: Genesis 1:3 (R.S.V.)—" 'Let there be light'; and there was light"—and Luke 22:41–44 (R.S.V.)—"And he withdrew from them about a stone's throw, and knelt down and prayed, 'Father, if thou art willing, remove

this cup from me; nevertheless not my will, but thine, be done.' . . . And being in an agony he prayed more earnestly; and his sweat became like great drops of blood falling down upon the ground." Dr. Temple said that in those two quotations there is depicted the difference for God between creating the universe with all its millions of stars, and the making of a selfish soul into a loving one. To create was easy; but convert hearts like ours from self-centeredness into the love which is God's own nature, that costs the agony and the bloody sweat and the death upon the cross. Recall the welcome Palestinian people gave Jesus' concept of the Great Society as long as Jesus was instrumental in creating changes to their advantage. Recall also the resistance, opposition, and hostility he incurred when he insisted that nothing of permanent value could be achieved until men and women individually were prepared to open their lives to God and allow their lives to be used in the service of God's kingdom. Sooner or later we either go into submission to God's loving purpose or into collision with it.

2) What Calvary exposes. God shows and clearly proves his own love for us by the fact that while we were still sinners Christ died for us. (a) Now, as then, we are still sinners because we are rebels against God and try to wreck his purposes for the world and for our personal lives. The cost to us may be much; the cost to God is infinitely great. A man whose uncontrollable temper wrecks his future and family relationships, a nation that permits and practices racial discrimination, an economic system that enriches the relatively few at the expense of the many may be cruel in themselves, but the deepest sin lies in their frustration of God's great design for his human family. Christ on the cross exposes the tragic reality of human sin. (b) The cross induces despair as the ugly fact of sin is thrown into glaring light. But the good news of God in Christ is a gospel of hope. The cross demonstrates the lengths and depths and height and breadth of divine love. Our Lord knew that men would only discover life through his death. Said staunch Protestant theologian James Denney to a Scottish congregation, "I wish I could hold up a crucifix to you, and say 'God loves like that!' " Don't think of sin only in personal terms, although you may begin with your own failure. I am part of the problem and sin of the social conditions which continue to crucify God's purposes for the world. And don't defer your repentance for your

rebellion and estrangement. Receive God's forgiveness and accept your commission from him. Then you may, as Paul wrote, ". . . exult in God through our Lord Jesus, through whom we have now been granted reconciliation" (Romans 5:11, N.E.B.).

## Christ's affluent society

TEXT: *"For in union with Christ you have become rich in all things, including all speech and all knowledge"* (*1 Corinthians 1:5, T.E.V.*).

Professor John K. Galbraith of Harvard has been credited with coining the phrase, "the affluent society." Despite tragic "pockets" of poverty against which we are urged to make war, this describes our North American society. True, its limits and limitations evoke uneasiness in thoughtful citizens and religious leaders. Nevertheless, most of us are like the apocryphal woman who wrote the federal government: "Where is the welfare state everybody talks about? I want to move into it."

To some it may seem revolting to speak of "Christ's affluent society." Nevertheless, the New Testament speaks more than once of the riches of Christ, the wealth that Christ's people find in their friendship with him. Here is Paul, himself undoubtedly financially poor, perhaps half-blind, compelled to work at a humble trade to make both ends meet. Probably he was buried in a pauper's grave when he was executed by Roman government order. He declares that in everything we are enriched by Christ.

Read 1 Corinthians 1:4–9, T.E.V., the section headed "Blessings in Christ (p. 370), and you will read the Apostle's thanksgiving for the sterling qualities in his correspondents, the members of First Church, Corinth. God's grace had given them uncommon ability to discuss the faith in knowledge of its deeper meaning. This is no mean endowment or attainment. In a fiercely skeptical, controversial society such as ours today, it is the mark of a church rich in faith and intellectual power to be able to discuss, expound, and uphold the Christian faith. Significantly, Paul says nothing about other essential forms of Christian wealth such as love and unity. The Corinthian

Christians were weaker in these. Nevertheless, he thanks God for this fruit of the Spirit of which his own preaching and teaching had been the root. "Thank God," he is saying, "the testimony, the teaching is proved to have been vital and valid."

What are elements in Christian affluence? A thoughtful Christian once suggested some of these elements as he recalled how his union with Christ enriched Paul with the very possessions which he seemed to have lacked. Is there something useful in citing some of these? (1) Although denied (as far as we know) the wonderful enrichment of married love, this man who voluntarily chose to devote himself completely to the proclamation of the gospel and the founding of churches sublimated this God-given instinct. "The Son of God," he writes, ". . . loved me, and gave himself for me." "The love of Christ," he explains in another place, "controls me." Cardinal Newman observed that Paul "had a thousand friends, and loved each as his own soul. . . ."

2) Homeless, he found through Christ and his service of Christ many homes where he was warmly welcomed. Lois, Eunice, and young Timothy gave him a home at Lystra; Priscilla and Aquila welcomed him to their home in Corinth; Rufus and his aged mother made him a home in their home in Rome. "In every way . . . enriched in him."

3) Through Christ and in Christ's community Paul had the joy of affectionate children. True, they were, as he would say, his "spiritual children," but upon them he poured his love. To Galatian Christians he speaks with great yearning and tenderness. When he speaks to the Corinthian church folk he says, "I speak as to my children." To his junior partner he says, "Timothy, my own son!" When he pleads with Philemon for a runaway slave, he speaks of the slave as "Onesimus, who is my own son in Christ; for while in prison I became his spiritual father."

4) What of the priceless treasure Paul found and which we, like so many others, can find: the meaning of life—the motivation for great living—God gives us in Christ? "To me to live is Christ." As Moffatt translates one of Paul's affirmations: "Life means Christ to me" (Philippians 1:21). *Today's English Version* underlines the fact even more dramatically: "For what is life? To me, it is Christ!" "For in union with Christ you have become"—or you can become—"rich in all things."

## Making God very great

TEXT: ". . . *as the scripture says,*
*'What no man ever saw or heard,*
*'What no man ever thought could happen,*
*'Is the very thing God prepared for those who love him'* "
(*1 Corinthians* 2:9, T.E.V.).

A devout but uneducated Christian woman attended the profound Gifford Lectures at Edinburgh, Scotland, delivered by Niebuhr. These lectures were later published as *The Nature and Destiny of Man.** Asked her opinion of them she said modestly, "I did not understand much of it, but I do know that he made God very great." In the Apostle Paul's discussion of wisdom he makes the above free quotation or paraphrase of Isaiah 64:4 and 65:17. It is good to proclaim greatness of the God whose self-disclosure in the Lord Jesus Christ is the Good News. A gifted older preacher asked to speak to university students spoke on "Three Things I Know About God." These were the three: (1) God awakens us (Ephesians 5:14). (2) God enlightens us (John 1:18). (3) God empowers us (Colossians 1:11). All we need do, says Paul, is to love the One who will reveal "what no man ever saw or heard, what no man ever thought could happen."

## God—dead or alive?

TEXT: (*1 Corinthians 8:4–7, T.E.V.*)

On November 8, 1965, virtually all of the northeastern portion of the United States and a small area of eastern Canada were plunged into darkness by an unprecedented electric power failure. In some places communities were deprived of light, heat, and power.

In the 1960's a few professors of religion—including one who occupies a chair of theology in a theological seminary—announced their conviction that God is dead. One of these so-called "radical theologians," Professor Thomas J. J. Altizer,

* (New York: Charles Scribner's Sons, 1953).

said that he believes that we should not only accept the fact of God's death but will the death of God! The news caused some to be plunged into darkness.

Is God dead or alive? A majority opinion one way or the other will not demonstrate his existence or nonexistence. With many others we believe that God is alive, that, in the paraphrase of a pre-Christian Greek thinker, there is no place where God is not present.

What can we say as we face this basic issue?

1) We can try to ascertain what our "Christian atheists" mean by their phrase "death of God." Professor Harmon R. Holcomb, a colleague of one of the death-of-God theologians, has examined all the literature produced by the American exponents of the view. He reports that the phrase is used in six different ways, "with one and the same author frequently wobbling among the six." * At times they seem to mean that the prevailing concept of God is dead; at other times they do not. Whimsically, Professor Holcomb says, "We shall need God's own help in locating what they clearly mean." However, after examining their statements, he concludes, as does this writer, that they mean what they say. God for them is not only absent to secular man, not only not experienced and not needed; God is dead. Writes Professor William Hamilton, "It is really that we do not know, do not adore, do not possess, do not believe in God. It is not just that a capacity has dried up within us; we do not take all this as merely a statement about our frail psyches, we take it as a statement about the nature of the world and we try to convince others. God is dead." †

2) How did our "God is dead" theologians get that way? Professor Langdon B. Gilkey is sure that tracing the influences which led them to their conclusion may be a long, complex study. Certainly they owe some of their emphases to Paul Tillich, Karl Barth, Rudolf Bultmann, and most of all to the German martyr, Dietrich Bonhoeffer. We may also cite the culture and society of our time. Technological, urban, secular influences have had tremendous impact upon many. "Man-talk" has certainly replaced "God-talk" in everyday living for a majority of persons.

* Harmon R. Holcomb, in a privately printed paper, "The Language of Worship in a Secular Age," Colgate Rochester Divinity School, 1960, pp. 13 ff.
† *The Christian Scholar*, vol. XLVIII, no. 1, p. 31

3) Does this mean that there is likely to be a large-scale desertion from the Christian forces of sincere, honest "Christian atheists"? It is highly unlikely. Edmund Burke was sure that no fair man indicts an entire nation. Similarly we cannot indict an entire theological seminary because one or two out of a score of teachers repudiate belief in God, loyalty to the church, even though the "Christian atheists" (some of them) inconsistently and wistfully wish to retain Jesus Christ at least as a "place" or "location" and urge obedience to Jesus. The faithful Christian, shocked by learning a teacher of Christian theology has moved into radical denial of Christian theism, should not yield to neurotic panic or angrily demand that such apostates or heretics be "fired." Our seminaries have constructive Christian theologians. Meanwhile, we who affirm belief in one God, the Father, and our Lord, Jesus Christ our Savior, must manifest something of God's graciousness and love toward those who attack our faith.

4) We can thank our radical theologians for shaking us out of our lethargic, tepid acceptance of the central Christian belief. We should be grateful that we are stimulated to think things through and to think more deeply concerning our "ultimate concern." It may be true, as more than one keen thinker has remarked, that relatively few of our contemporaries ask as did Martin Luther, "How can I find a gracious God?" More often they ask in the sweat and struggle of the social revolutions of our time, "How can I find a gracious neighbor?" How long will neighbors or we ourselves be gracious without experiencing God's love?

5) There must be positive response to the challenge of those who claim God is dead. Radical doubt and radical denial must be met with radical faith in the living God. We must give our reasons for our faith and demonstrate its validity in our actions and lives. While we thank the radical theologians for the turbulence of mind they have brought, we must say "No thank you" when they ask us to accept a secular statement of faith. We need not only Christ as teacher, as a "place," but as God-in-a-human-life, present and empowering. He is the "man for others" and the man for God, and the God become man for us men and our salvation.

We learn that Friedrich Nietzsche first coined the phrase, that he may have borrowed it from Hegel. One United

Church of Christ writer says that Hegel took the phrase from a Lutheran passion hymn by Johannes Rist which celebrates the death of the God-man on Calvary. But Christ who died was raised from the dead. The Christlike God is alive forevermore, and we may know him, experience his love, and do his will. ". . . yet for us there is one God, the Father, from whom all being comes, towards whom we move; and there is one Lord, Jesus Christ, through whom all things came to be, and we through him" (1 Corinthians 8:6, N.E.B.).

## Christians are in this fraternity

TEXT: "*All of you, then, are Christ's body, and each one is a part of it. In the church, then, God has put all in place: in the first place, apostles, in the second place, prophets, and in the third place, teachers; then those who perform miracles, followed by those who are given the power to heal, or to help others, or to direct them, or to speak with strange sounds*" (*1 Corinthians* 12:27, 28).

1) Christians belong to a fraternity? Yes, and while there are no secrets except "open" secrets, it is indeed a blood brotherhood. The life of Christ was poured out that we might become members of his spiritual body. Moreover, says the greatest exponent of the Faith in the New Testament church, God has put all of us in some particular place in this fraternity. One name for us comes low on the list. Just because it occurs fifth does not mean that those who are in this place are fifth-rate. Far from it; every loyal follower of Christ in the first or twentieth century is one of these. We are to be "helpers," says the Apostle.

2) To be a helper in the Christian sense is to be given the grace of helping by the Spirit himself. To try harder than the non-Christian is not only exhausting, it proves futile when helping is disdained or opposed. Only divine grace can make and keep us ordinary folk helpers.

3) If we like dividing people into two classes, there are those who are always ready to help and those who are never ready or willing to help. You know what type of person we value most.

4) To help "without any thought of reward save that we know we do" our Lord's will, still brings deep, durable satisfaction. Professor William Barclay told the story of the famous parson and poet, George Herbert. On his way to a meeting of a little group of friends who played together in what today's youngster would call a "combo," he passed a driver whose wagon or cart got stuck in a muddy ditch. Immediately George Herbert went to work to help the unfortunate driver extricate the cart. Both working together, they succeeded but only when Herbert was almost literally plastered with mud and very late for his meeting. When he arrived he explained his appearance and why he was so late. "You are too late now," said one of his fellow musicians. "You have missed the music." "Yes," said George Herbert, quietly, "but I shall have songs at midnight."

When you and I look back across our day, will there not be some deep joy in the thought that we have tried to help and not hinder our fellows? We can and often do pass by on the other side. When we use God's gift and serve others as helpers we do have songs in the night and in the day, too. It's a simple brotherhood, this brotherhood of Christ's helpers of others. We belong, if we are Christ's.

## Are good manners obsolete in a time of stress?

TEXT: ". . . *love is not ill-mannered, or selfish, or irritable; love does not keep a record of wrongs. . . .*"
(*1 Corinthians 13:5, T.E.V.*).

Are good manners obsolete in a time of stress such as the present? Many appear to think so. Abruptness, down-right rudeness, even savage retorts to those thought to be prejudiced, wrong, blind, are evident even among those who "profess and call themselves Christian." In times of crisis it may seem sound to say that we haven't time for the little courtesies and niceties of a more stable, courtly society. What is needed and wanted by our minority groups is not politeness but justice. But can we not strive and sacrifice for justice and genuine brotherhood without sacrificing Christian manners? Jesus, our Lord, knew what it was to fight alert, vindictive opponents. He did use "abrasive" language against powerful groups. But he was moved more to sadness than to anger when he realized the plight of an entire urban community, his own city and nation's capital, Jerusalem. Someone noted that he treated a proven prostitute with exquisite courtesy. Howard Thurman once said that Christ loved Mary of Magdala into newness of life.

1) Good manners are never obsolete for a follower of Jesus. He left us an example in this also, that we should follow him.

2) Good manners are an expression of the respect and concern for others, however "different" or "difficult," which is Christlike love. "Love is patient and kind . . . love is not ill-mannered, or selfish, or irritable; love does not keep a record of wrongs. . . ." After an internationally eminent organizer of minority groups had given lectures at one of our seminaries, a reviewer made a significant criticism. He appreciated this leader's contributions but challenged one tenet which consciously lies behind the social worker's operations. This is his belief that hate must always accompany love. Such love, the church contends, has always been extended—or must be extended—to "enemy" as well as to "neighbor."

3) Good manners in the deep Christian sense of loving the enemy or the unlovable person is one of the Spirit's agents for turning an enemy into a friend. We are to "speak the truth in love," wrote the Apostle Paul. It is the only way by which the truth will be received by one who may be hostile to it and to us.

One perceptive British Christian said: "Remembering all the beautiful and strong things enshrined in courtesy, I think if men would pledge themselves in utter loyalty to learn and practice courtesy in all the ways of life, we could afford to wait quite a long time for the mere political or economic expression of a change that, through courtesy, would have been wrought." This is no trivial, obsolescent matter. Hilaire Belloc summed up the matter in four lines:

*Of Courtesy, it is much less*
*Than Courage of Heart or Holiness.*
*Yet in my walks it seems to me*
*That the Grace of God is in Courtesy.**

* "Courtesy" by Hilaire Belloc in *Verses and Sonnets* (London: Harold Duckworth & Co., Ltd.). Reprinted by permission of A. D. Peters & Company.

## Is bad temper really bad?

TEXT: "*. . . love is not ill-mannered, or selfish, or irritable . . .*" (*1 Corinthians 13:5, T.E.V.*).

In the King James Version the phrase translated is "not easily provoked." This is the source of our word "paroxysm," which is a word associated with rage or a temper explosion. The Greek means "to sharpen." You put a point on something and then jab someone with it. Irritation in a really painful sense results. What Paul means is that the loving person is not provoked to anger. Is bad temper, anger, really bad?

1) Anger is sin when it is uncontrolled and misdirected. How many lives, families, church boards and congregations have been hurt because someone "blew a fuse," "blew his top," denounced others for what he considered injustice to himself!

2) Bad temper is bad because it is an immature way of dealing with a difficulty. When we become men and women this explosive type of response should be put away.

3) Bad temper is bad because it is self-centered. We would not be nearly as incensed if it were somebody else who had been neglected, unfairly treated, ignored. Jesus showed moral indignation. He blazed out, but never against insults or injuries done to himself. To read the Gospels is to realize that two things aroused his anger: misrepresentation of the holy, just, and loving Father whom he revealed and served and man's inhumanity to man (see Mark 3:1–6).

Most often our bad temper or anger is a selfish, egotistic passion. Henry Drummond, nineteenth-century teacher of science in Scotland and friend and co-worker of Dwight L. Moody, once observed that bad temper did more harm than intemperance. Of course these two sins frequently go together.

4) What is the cure? Is it oversimplified to say love learned in the school of Christ? Such love will enable us to deal with the strain and stress, illness or frustration which frequently explodes in bad temper. Such love will also enable us to be "never irritated, never resentful." A hymn speaks of Jesus' unwearied forgiveness in the face of foes who hated, despised, reviled him, and of friends who "unfaithful prove." It concludes with a prayer for "hearts to love like Thee, O Lord, to grieve / Far more for others' sins, than all / The wrongs that we receive" (written by Edward Denny, 1796–1889).

[132]

## "Is marriage dying, too?"

TEXT: (*1 Corinthians 13, T.E.V.*).

This is the chapter heading in a wise, witty, and unconventional book by Earl H. Brill.*

Scripture might well be 1 Corinthians 13 which will "bite" into our hearers' minds more if, instead of the familiar translations, we use the American Bible Society's *Good News for Modern Man.* Consider this rendition of verse 7 which reads: "Love never gives up: its faith, hope, and patience never fail."

1) A considerable number of persons incline to think that Christian, monogamous, lifetime marriage is dying along with other once vital and apparently enduring institutions, beliefs, and practices. In the United States the casualty list of those marriages which end in divorce remains appalling. Moreover, many marriages persist in name only. Love may never fail, but obviously love was not an active ingredient in many marriages which are failing.

2) Marriage is not dying even if some marriages have died. Says Dr. Brill, reassuringly, "Have no fear that marriage will disappear. You may be sure that even with pressure off, most young people will probably decide to get married just the same." †

3) We may well see real and sometimes radical changes in marriage. It will no longer be regarded as "a success symbol." We shall also realize that marriage is not to be considered "the cure for everything from boredom to psychosis." Moreover, we must not expect too much from fallible, sinful human beings just because they have been legally married in a church ceremony. Above all, there must be readiness for marriage. Perhaps the suggestion is not wild that "one way to deal with divorce is to make the grounds for marriage stiffer."

4) Allowing for the importance of intelligent preparation for marriage, including sound knowledge of sex and sexuality, household economics, temperamental compatibility, and the rest, Christian marriage will live on and even increase as we learn what it is to love each other "in Christ." What about the love whose "faith, hope and patience never fail"?

* *Sex Is Dead and Other Postmortems* (New York: The Seabury Press, Inc., 1967.

† *Ibid.*, p. 37.

## Any witnesses?

TEXT: "*I passed on to you what I received, which is of the greatest importance: that Christ died for our sins, as written in the Scriptures; that he was buried and raised to life on the third day . . . that he appeared . . .*" (*1 Corinthians 15:3–5, T.E.V.*).

Some years ago an eloquent and influential Christian preacher was the Negro woman pastor of a church in Raleigh, North Carolina. Biblical, relevant, evangelistic, she had done much to move white citizens to act on behalf of social justice for the black community. From time to time during her sermon she would declare one of the Christian truths, then pause, and ask, not rhetorically, "Any witnesses?" If members of the congregation seemed reluctant to testify out of their personal experience, she would call upon persons known to her and wait for their response. In this tremendous section of his "encyclical" to the Corinthian church of long ago, the Apostle Paul is answering the question which many since have asked concerning the Christian claim that Jesus Christ was "raised to life on the third day"—any reliable witnesses? any evidence? That there are discrepancies in the documents, no one may deny. That the first Christians held the invincible belief that their Master had conquered physical and every other kind of death is equally clear. Any witnesses?

1) There is the existence of the Christian church. One New Testament scholar, Dr. A. M. Hunter of Aberdeen, Scotland, expresses it thus: "Had the Crucifixion ended the disciples' fellowship with Jesus, it is hard to see how the Church could have come into existence, and harder still to see how it could have continued these nineteen hundred years." In our revolutionary era the institutional church is undergoing, and will continue to undergo, many changes, but the church, the body of Christ, the worshiping, witnessing, serving and redemptive community of Christ's people, will continue and ultimately triumph as God's servant.

2) The existence of the Christian scriptures. Who would have bothered to write the New Testament documents if Jesus' career had ended as a crucified revolutionary? Remember that every word in the New Testament was written by men who believed in the risen Lord. The learned theologian James Denny

was convinced that the New Testament itself, not Jesus' appearing in Jerusalem or Galilee, or the empty tomb, is the primary evidence for the Resurrection.

3) The existence of the Lord's day. True, "the secular city" (and the secular countryside, for that matter) now has transformed the first day of the week from a holy day to a holiday, but millions still celebrate the worship of the living God on what is still known in some circles as the Lord's day. It is highly improbable that any Christian Jew would have changed the sacred day from the Sabbath (Saturday) to "the first day of the week" (Acts 20:7; 1 Corinthians 16:2; Revelation 1:10) except for the reason given, that on this day the risen Lord was first seen.

4) There is the personal experience of the risen Lord. "Last of all," said Paul, and you sense the excitement in his soul as he wrote or dictated the words, "he appeared also to me. . . ." The life of the risen Christ has vitalized and transformed countless men and women and boys and girls. With the Resurrection, the kingdom, God's fatherly rule, came with power.

This is why the twentieth-century historian T. R. Glover of Cambridge University, England, could write: "The Gospels are not four, but ten thousand times ten thousand, and thousands of thousands, and the last word of every one of them is, 'Lo, I am with you alway, even unto the end of the world.' " *

## Examine the evidence

TEXT: " . . . *he was buried and raised to life on the third day. . . . Then he appeared . . .*" (*1 Corinthians 15:4, 6,* T.E.V.).

*The Easter message is based on the five New Testament accounts of the Resurrection of Jesus:* (1) *1 Corinthians 15:3–8;* (2) *Mark 16;* (3) *Matthew 28;* (4) *Luke 24;* (5) *John 20, 21.*

* *The Conflict of Religions in the Early Roman Empire* (London: Metheun and Company, 1919), p. 140.

One New Testament student is convinced that the truths which emerge from the Resurrection story are five: (1) He is alive; death could not hold him. (2) He meets his followers in everyday places: in a garden; in rooms where they had already met; on the road; at a supper table; by the lake shore—never on the clouds. (3) He breaks through fears and sends the transformed followers out to complete his task. (4) He interprets God's design of redemption throughout all history. (5) He gives life (see Romans 6:4–11; 1 Corinthians 15:20–22; Colossians 2:12, 13, and 3:1–4). Physical death will overtake us but eternal life has begun here and now. "We have passed from death to life."

Easter is not a vague rejoicing that springtime has returned; nor is it a festival of immortality for every human being. Easter is the cosmic response to the faith, the life and love and death of Jesus Christ. It is an experience which makes Christians cry "Alleluia!"

## Fund for Christians

TEXT: "*Now the matter about the money to be raised to help God's people in Judea: you must do what I told the churches in Galatia to do. On the first day of every week each of you must put aside some money, in proportion to what he has earned, and save it up so there will be no need to collect money when I come*" (*1 Corinthians 16:1, 2, T.E.V.*).

Funds for one good cause or another are familiar features of our society. Not every human need is met by a benevolent government. To a few otherwise sensible souls, it seems the church talks too much about money; it seems unspiritual, mundane, too "this worldly." However, even such spiritual-minded saints may be persuaded that there is such a thing as a healthy Christian materialism. As someone has said, Christ is concerned not just about soul salvation but about whole salvation—of body, mind, spirit. The incarnation of God in a material, human body forever sanctified material things.

1) Every day is a stewardship day for Christians. True,

most churches designate a Sunday in the fall as Stewardship Sunday. Paul reminds the Christians that "On the first day of every week" (R.S.V.) we are to put something aside so that God's work may proceed into God's world, in God's time and space.

Impulse-giving is a phrase known to economists, store managers, professional fund raisers. IBM's *Think* magazine (January–February 1965) had a discussion of why people give. Four reasons were cited: (a) *Impulsive buying* for small, unimportant items. (Some people contribute to the church as if it were in such a category!) (b) *Habit buying* of routine items such as groceries. (c) *Calculated buying* of large articles such as a car, a refrigerator, a home. (d) *Nonrational buying* involving bargains or emergencies. To lay aside something on the first day of every week may result in habitual, calculated, stewardship giving.

2) Contributing regularly and sacrificially to the Fund for Christians is an almost infallible indication of the kind of person you are. A man whose literary labors were devoted to biographies of famous persons said that the surest way to find out what kind of a man any man was is to examine the stubs of his checkbooks. What a person gives money for tells the real story of his character and gives helpful clues as to the kind of life he lived. What you give week by week, not only to admirable special causes, but to the cause of Christ, tells how much you care about what matters most.

Halford E. Luccock related to his students the story of the mass baptism of a savage tribe of Franks. It was in the Dark Ages and these candidates for Christian discipleship were proud, professional warriors. To make sure they could continue to engage in fighting, many of them went into the water holding their battle axes out of the water as they were immersed. Then they could say, "This hand has never been baptized," arguing that it could be swung again in slaughter of enemies. Dr. Luccock wondered if many of us didn't hold our pocketbooks and checkbooks on high as if to proclaim, "This has never been baptized!"

3) Our contributions to Christians and to the Christian mission are basic to Christian living. Our gifts not only maintain Christ's work in our world, but they symbolize, express and deepen our Christian love and unity. To be a Christian

is to care; to care is to share. To share is to *spend helpfully all resources everywhere.*

## Marching orders for Christ's forces

TEXT: "*Be alert, stand firm in the faith, be brave, be strong. Do all your work in love.*" (*1 Corinthians 16:13, 14, T.E.V.*).

The Apostle Paul's first four directives in this chapter sound like those which might be issued by a commander of troops in a battle area. As William Barclay paraphrased it: "As a sentinel, be ever on the alert. When under attack, stand fast in the faith, and yield not an inch. In time of battle, play a hero's part. Like a well-equipped and well-trained soldier, be strong to fight for your divine Commander." Like it or not, all who are Christians are members of a salvation army. We are under orders. Certainly we are in a world which in various ways tries to destroy our cause, often by efforts to contain the church within an area the world calls "religious."*

In First Corinthians, an earlier exponent of Christ's gospel addresses himself to the same question. He has his answer: (1) "Be alert." Know the strength of the opposition, the needs of the areas now occupied by enemies of Christ's kind of living. Knowledge of our culture and our own community is needed. Awareness of the kind and strength of the opposition can make us intelligent, effective warriors of the Spirit. (2) " . . . stand firm in your faith . . . " that is, in your conviction respecting man's relationship to God and to God's design for mankind. This also means: confide yourself and your cause into God's keeping. We may fail him; he never fails us. (3) " . . . be brave, be strong." Act like men, like Christ's men and women. Let Christ communicate his valor to you. Inner reinforcement from God's Spirit turns rabbits into lions! Mark was probably the young man wrapped in a linen cloth who ran away when soldiers arrested Jesus (see Mark 14:51, 52). Mark also defected when the going became tough and rough on his mission with Paul. But the symbol of Mark now is a lion. Legend says he

* See *How the Church Can Minister to the World without Losing Itself,* by Langdon Gilkey (New York: Harper & Row, 1964).

was dragged through the streets of his episcopal city to his martyrdom. Says the writer of Psalm 31:24 (R.S.V.): "Be strong, and let your heart take courage, all you who wait for the Lord!" In other words, wait on the Lord of life and your heart will take courage. (4) "Do all your work in love." What is love? Paul Tillich comes close to the New Testament meaning: "love is the urge to reunite the separated." This love is Christlike love inspired by God's love for us.

## "No gravel in the face!"

TEXT: *"He helps us in all our troubles, so that we are able to help those who have all kinds of troubles, using the same help that we ourselves have received from God"* (*2 Corinthians 1:4, T.E.V.*).

William Barclay told the story of a man who left a certain congregation. Asked why, he referred to the preacher who was reputed to have a talent for denunciation. "I was tired," said the man, "of getting handfuls of gravel flung in my face every Sunday."

1) It is the duty of Christ's faithful herald to afflict the comfortable. Too often, our resistance to needed social change, as in the area of racial justice and reconciliation, expresses itself in sighing for more comforting sermons. One of Christ's first gifts is a cross, a shouldered burden. Crosses are hard, heavy, uncomfortable. We must accord Christ's preachers freedom to be prophetic in the biblical meaning of prophetic. The church must be the enlightened conscience of the community.

2) It is also true that Christ's transmitters must comfort the afflicted. "If I had my ministry to do over again," a once famous preacher, Dr. R. W. Dole, said, "I would preach more comforting sermons." We would like to know what he meant by "comforting." Most men and women fight hard battles with their own personal problems, fears, guilts, burdens imposed by caring for others, handicaps, sickness. "Never morning wore to evening but some heart did break." What do you give for a broken heart, a distraught mind, a lacerated spirit? We give them Christ. Rather, Christ gives himself to them through us.

3) How is God "the all-merciful Father, the God whose comfort (consolation) never fails us"? He identifies with us, he goes through it with us, he companions us up our lesser Calvaries into the resurrection.

4) God's comfort is given us that we may comfort others. Only the wounded in life's battle can be the healers. "Comfort" means "strong together with"—whom? God in Christ. Still he calls: "Come unto me, all ye that labour and are heavy laden, and I will give you rest" (Matthew 11:28, K.J.V.), not rest from labor, but rest in labor; not rest from all struggle and all suffering, but rest—comfort, strength—in them.

## Believing is seeing

TEXT: *"But it is removed, as the scripture says; 'Moses' veil was removed when he turned to the Lord' "* (*2 Corinthians 3:16*, T.E.V.).

An eminent theologian of the early twentieth century was the late John Oman. Among his influential theological books was *Vision and Authority*.* In this profound study Dr. Oman wrote that in the human situation God seems to have created four barriers to seeing into the mystery of God. These are the veils of ignorance, of sin, of weakness, and of what Oman called evanescence or the process of vanishing. Dr. Oman then said that in Jesus Christ and in the Christian religion these veils are removed. Here are Oman's words: "Enshrouded by these four veils man stands before the mystery of God. By four great Christian doctrines they are taken away. The veil of our ignorance is removed by the Incarnation, the veil of our sin by the Atonement, the veil of our weakness by Grace, the veil of our evanescence by Immortality.† Here is a fourfold outline of the essence of Christianity. In making these glorious truths clear we turn almost inevitably to some of the great affirmations of scripture: (1) John 1:14, John 14:9; (2) Romans 5:11 and the entire fifth chapter of Romans; (3) Hebrew 4:16, 2 Corinthians 12:9, Ephesians 2:5, 8; (4) 2 Timothy 1:10, John 3:16, John 6:40, 47.

Professor William Barclay's comment is pertinent: ". . . left to ourselves, we are bound to live a life in which the

* (New York: Harper & Row, Publishers, 1929).
† *Ibid.*, p. 231.

inevitable veils of humanity conceal God from us; but in Jesus the veils are removed, and we see God as he is, rejoicing in our new-found friendship with him, triumphant in the power in which our weakness becomes his strength, certain that after life here there is still greater life, both for us and for those whom we love."*

## A great word for a tough year

TEXT: ". . . *there are many enemies, but we are never without a friend* . . ." (*2 Corinthians* 4:9, *T.E.V.*).

So this New Year is likely to be a tough one? With the Vietnam war still raging and our cities boiling under the lids clamped down to prevent anarchy, chaos, and death; with the generation gap widening between parents and children; with the war against poverty often bogged down; with Black Power being recognized as an inescapable element in the total power structure—what else could it be but tough? Has it ever been anything else for realistic Christians aware of the evil in human beings and in their society? Did our Lord ever hide a cross to win a follower? "In the world you will have trouble," he said.

This year of grace on which we have launched will have its crises, its crosses, its conflicts. This, then, is the first incontrovertible fact: (1) It will be a tough, rough, critical year. Christians are aware of the ethical and spiritual issues which others may not see. Christians are always torn between what should be and what is. Christians must live with the tension created by the disparity between the ideal and the actual. ". . . there are many enemies . . ." said Paul of his own society and personal situation. He was not paranoiac, not suffering from unwarranted feelings of persecution. We, too, have enemies. Some may be personal; most of our enemies operate through persons or groups of persons but under the names of resistance to needed change, or bigotry, or pride, or greed, or contempt for "lesser breeds without the law." Moreover, within each of us are enemies of our moral and spiritual health, subversives that destroy our courage, our faith, our sense of

* *Seen in the Passing* (London: William Collins Sons & Co., Ltd., 1966), p. 158.

what is vital. It was no overstatement: ". . . there are many enemies . . ."

2) ". . . there are many enemies . . ." but that is not the whole picture of the year and years ahead. ". . . there are many enemies . . ." but we are never without a friend. "What would be the most wonderful thing in the world you could have?" asked a fatherly soul of a little girl. She answered with wisdom beyond her years: "To have a real friend." God gives us real friends; we never deserve or earn them. Paul may have been thinking of a loyal younger colleague such as Timothy. Certainly within Christ's company, the church, we have a friend, and more than a friend. The noble name of those commonly called Quakers should be an accurate description of every congregation of God's people: the Religious Society of Friends. Within the redeeming community of Christians we have friends who may know all about us—our sins, our weaknesses, our blunders—and still believe in us. Of course there are unfriendly, censorious, unloving persons within the church. One twelfth of our Lord's company was untrustworthy, a schemer and traitor. Nevertheless, take them all in all, Christ's folk are more likely to accept us, support us, love us than any group in society.

3) "We are never without a friend" describes the place of Jesus Christ in our lives. We may find it sentimental and otherwise distasteful to sing, "What a friend we have in Jesus." Nevertheless, men and women of heroic spirit have found the spiritual companionship of the living Lord a source of strength and healing nothing else equals. To keep our friendship with Christ in repair we need to do the things he asks us. In a tough year in a rough world this is the faith, this is the fact which makes us adequate for anything that may come. In the words of a layman which deeply affected the life of one who heard him make the simple prayer, "Lord, we are thankful thou art able." With him we are able too, for anything the year may bring.

## Christians, for a change?

TEXT: "*When anyone is joined to Christ he is a new being: the old is gone, the new has come*" (*2 Corinthians 5:17,* T.E.V.) (*See also 2 Peter 3:11–13 and Isaiah 43:14,* R.S.V.)

## [142] Christians, for a change?

One summer a churchwoman attended a school conducted by the synod of her denomination in Troy, N.Y. She was much impressed by the theme: "Christians for a Change" or "Christians, for a Change." She and her fellow students were informed of the tremendous and rapid changes caused by population and knowledge explosions, in technological fields, etc. In such a changing society two questions confronted them. First, "Can we be Christians for a change, when this means moving out of 'the four, neat walls of our individual churches'?" Second, facing the question in its other form, "Can we be Christians if we limit our witness and study, our practice and friendliness to one hour of worship in church each week?"

1) Being human, Christians tend to resist change. Alan Pryce-Jones, British writer and one-time editor of the *Times Literary Supplement* of London, explains why in middle age he decided to change careers and countries. "I think," he writes, "that what most had depressed me about England was its resistance to change. From 1929 onwards it was clear that the old order was in permanent eclipse." But thirty years later "the subsoil was entirely undisturbed. The world in which my countrymen live—the world of the 1960s—is primed by a national heart still restricted to the rhythms of 1880."*

Is this not the case with many of us in North America?

2) Some changes need to be resisted. Certain values remain constant, however changed their expression. "Now abideth. . . ."

3) Christians are expected to welcome changes which make for the doing of God's will as this is disclosed in Christ. Our God is the God of dynamic change. "Behold, I do a new thing, saith the Lord." "If any one is in Christ, he is a new creation." Life-changing and world-changing are capsule descriptions of our goals as Christ's servants, and as Christ's servant church. "Change and decay in all around I see," moans the timid Christian. But "He who would valiant be 'gainst all disaster," as John Bunyan said, must follow the Master. This Master ". . . is the same yesterday, today, and for ever . . ." (Hebrews 13:8), but he is forever ready to go further (Luke 24:28) because he is going further. His commands are "Come,"

* "A Late Transplant: Why I Left London for New York," *Harper's Magazine*, August, 1966, p. 12.

"Abide," "Go!" As his men and women we are able to be Christians for a change in our racial relationships, in our action for international peace and justice, in our programs for a more abundant life for the half of our world which now has not enough to eat. With his grace we can be in our family life, in our jobs, in our recreation, in our citizenship, Christians—for a change.

## Don't settle for anything less

TEXT: (*2 Corinthians 5:19; 1 Corinthians 15:3; Philippians 2:9, T.E.V.*).

Archibald M. Hunter quotes from a letter written by *British Weekly* editor Sir William Robertson Nicoll. The letter was written to James Denney. "I do not believe," wrote Nicoll, "that the Christian religion, let alone the Christian Church, can live, unless we can be sure of three things—a real being of God in Christ, the atoning death, and the exaltation of Christ."* Nicoll may have been a theological conservative, but he was no obscurantist or ranting extremist. Are these the essentials? Actually, many would be willing to reduce basic Christianity to possession of the spirit of Christ: having Christ's gentle, undiscourageable love toward everyone. One religious teacher is sure that love alone is enough, and a love without faith in a divine source of such love; love which is directed toward one's fellows without hope of any future beyond this dimension of existence. Nevertheless, the church "on the main line," classical Christianity, has said, "don't settle for less than these affirmations of the Apostle Paul: 'God was in Christ,' 'Christ died for our sins,' 'Therefore God has highly exalted him.' "

1) "A real being of God in Christ." This is surely the heart of the Good News: "God was in Christ reconciling the world to himself." Somehow, the infinite and eternal God made himself uniquely known in all that we mean when we say our Lord Jesus Christ. This universe is not "going it blind," it means intensely and it means good; God has acted decisively for us men and for our salvation in Jesus Christ.

2) "Christ died for our sins" is the second element in

* See *Teaching and Preaching the New Testament* (Philadelphia: The Westminster Press, 1963), p. 113.

basic Christianity. The cross today as in the first days of the church is a stumbling block to many. How can we be "saved" by the sacrificial death of a good and great person of long ago? If there is a God of love, will he not forgive us anyway? Isn't the important thing to face our failures, doing what we can to reduce their unfortunate effects, and then forgiving ourselves and forgiving those who have enjured us? No, it is not enough. Somehow, the "strange Man on the Cross" makes God's forgiveness real, available, effectual. We may never formulate an adequate theory of the Atonement; at the cross we know that Christ died for our sins and for the sins of the whole world, and we are made one with the divine love from which we had been separated and estranged by our willful wrongdoing.

3) ". . . For this reason God raised him to the highest place above . . . / So that . . . / All beings in heaven, and on earth, and in the world below / Will fall on their knees, / And all will openly proclaim that Jesus Christ is the Lord, / To the glory of God the Father" (Philippians 2:5–11). Theologians speak of "the exaltation of Christ" as meaning the resurrection, ascension, and continued presence in and among his own, of the Lord Jesus Christ. Surely the Apostle is declaring in this Philippian passage that the One who lived and taught and healed and was crucified by Roman troops on a Jewish hill is at the center of reality, alive and reigning, and destined to win the kingdoms of this world and of all other possible worlds. It doesn't look like it when you take a survey of our human situation. "Where is your Carpenter now?" asked the Roman friend of a Christian while both watched Christians being killed in the arena. "Making a coffin for your emperor," was the reply. "He must reign." He is reigning. Don't settle for less.

## Christmas in depth

TEXT: "*Our message is that God was making friends of all men through Christ. God did not keep an account of their sins against them, and he has given us the message of how he makes them his friends*" (*2 Corinthians 5:19, T.E.V.*).

"In depth" is a phrase getting considerable mileage in many areas. To come to church on Christmas Sunday or Christmas Day and have the meaning of Christmas discussed "in depth" may seem "just too much," or, as the woman said when she scanned the great Christmas hymns, "just too distressingly theological"! As a poetic columnist once wrote, Christmas celebrates carols, children, candy, and kindness. Of course; but is this all? Is the resurrection of Christ on the periphery of the Gospel or at its center? Without Christ's victory over death and evil there would have been no Christmas. Jesus Christ is "the man for us" because he was more than the best of men.

1) 2 Corinthians 5:19 is the shortest summary of basic Christianity our scriptures offer. It is the foundation of our religion. It is the New Testament expression of what is known as the doctrine of the Incarnation.

2) God and Christ are linked in Paul's affirmation, because God and Christ are inseparably joined in the mystery of the fact with which we have to do. God is not remote; having once pressed the button to start the "lift-off" of Creation he is not now on leave of absence from his universe. He humbled himself by living a completely human life of perfect obedience, even to the extent of dying. That is why Christmas is the best news. God was in Christ.

3) Because God was in Christ reconciling the world to himself we know that God is here in the tragedy and joy, in the perplexity and love of our human situation. "When . . . Quirinius was governor of Syria" God came in Jesus of Nazareth says Luke (2:2). Into a world of Roman governors, of taverns and "pubs," of carpenters and peasant mothers, shepherds and animals, rebels and nationalists, God came in a man. Today Quirinius is not governor. President Nixon and Queen Elizabeth and the leaders of the U.S.S.R., China, and other nations occupy the seats of the mighty. The Incarnation tells us that God is concerned with that. Christmas is more than at lyrical interlude in the pressures of business, more than a temporary escape from harsh realities.

In ancient Rome authorities once planned a magnificent procession. They selected one of the handsomest, most athletic young men, then covered him with gold leaf. It was so radiant and shining that as they marched around the city they discovered that before the day ended the young man was dead. Despite motion pictures of the James Bond variety, human beings are not meant to be covered with gold leaf. They cannot breathe if overlaid with gold plate. Too often something similar has been done to Jesus. We cover him with gold and tinsel, enthrone him on a pedestal, and feel that he and his way are irrelevant to our condition. Sometimes, being of a religious nature more or less, we smear the Christmas symbols with gold leaf of individualistic piety. Once a Woolworth store had a Nativity tableau in the window. One man seeing it exclaimed, "Good heavens! what next? They're even dragging religion into Christmas!" But the crib in the shop window captures the meaning of Christmas more than he thought. The Savior of the world is in the midst of the commercialism, the tinsel, the dirt, the cruelty and laughter and apathy of the thronging crowds. This is the world God in Christ came to save. This is the world we must work with him to remold. Gold wills to be incarnated into the total human situation. God wills to reconcile this world of secularity and sin and tears and dreams to himself.

The late John Baillie, theologian and World Council of Churches' leader, once quoted this same text and asked: "Would the people who see you daily, and with whom you have most to do, be able to guess, even if you had not told them, that you believe" this?

## Goodness gracious!

TEXT: *"For you know the grace of our Lord Jesus Christ: rich as he was, he made himself poor for your sake, in order to make you rich by his poverty"* (*2 Corinthians 8:9, T.E.V.*). (*See also James Moffatt's translation.*)

1) "Goodness gracious!" It sounds quaint, and to the "mod" generation antique; the kind of euphemism a grandparent might employ to express surprise. Reverse the words and we have something in short supply in all ages. Gracious goodness is what the New Testament means by love, the Christlike love which never condescends or makes the recipient feel like a welfare recipient. Dr. Alice Freeman Palmer, famous president of a great women's college, found herself in close relationship with other Christians who were "kind, but cold. There was no intentional freezing, but an absence of the sunshine which melts its own way." Another distinguished woman, a radiant and able Christian named Florence Allshorn (J. H. Oldham wrote her biography) told certain Christians she met

in East Africa, "You're all so good. Everywhere I go, everyone is up so early, so busy, so good." But she said that she sensed something vital was missing, what she called "the graciousness of goodness."

2) Gracious goodness must be the rule in our relationships with those whom we too easily describe as minority groups. Without oversimplifying complex and difficult tasks ahead of us, how can we move together toward justice with love unless we treat everyone as a human being? as a human being sensitive to the look in our eyes, the tone of our voice, the style of our lives?

3) To be a Christian is to care about persons and to care enough to help. How do we help them? There is uncommon insight into how caring becomes gracious goodness in Jeremiah 38. Ropes were let down to rescue the hapless victim. Jeremiah was sunk by his enemies in the mud of a waterless cistern. An Ethiopian called Ebedmelech deserves the medal of honor, for he not only pulled Jeremiah out before he died, but got some old rags and worn-out clothes out of a storehouse and lowered these by ropes, instructing Jeremiah to put them between his armpits and the ropes. This was being kind in a kindly way. The clothes prevented the ropes from hurting. How gracious is our goodness? Reinhold Niebuhr has said that most of the trouble in the world comes, not from evil people, but from people who consider themselves good.

4) Consider the graciousness of Jesus Christ. Jesus believed in a God and revealed a God who is utterly gracious. When Jesus told of the waiting Father who ran to meet his returning son ". . . while He was still a long way from home" (Luke 15:20), he was saying God is like that. He is a God of infinite grace and therefore of unsurpassed graciousness.

## Is your God too small?

TEXT: "*The grace of the Lord Jesus Christ, the love of God, and the fellowship of the Holy Spirit be with you all*" (*2 Corinthians 13:13, T.E.V.*).

Trinity Sunday, the first Sunday after Pentecost or Whitsunday, celebrates one of the most mysterious doctrines of the Christian faith. To many it is unintelligible, unnecessary and at best a kind of theological jigsaw puzzle. Nevertheless it was not remote when it was first formulated; it came straight out of the experience of ordinary Christians in the early church. Dr. J. B. Phillips' book title, *Your God Is Too Small,* was the indictment made, we hope graciously, by the first Christians to many of their fellows who felt they could define and delimit the infinite creator, redeemer, and sustainer of life. A famous Methodist leader, the late William E. Sangster, recalled a Trinity Sunday when he overhead a fourteen-year-old girl talk with three younger boys as they left church. Said the oldest boy, "I can't understand all this 'three in one and one in three' business." Replied the girl, "I can't understand it either, but I think of it this way. Mother is 'Mamma' to us; she is 'Mabel' to Daddy, and she is 'Mrs. Douglas' to lots of other people." Sangster knew that this is not the answer; the Trinity is more than a matter of names. Nowhere in the Bible is the doctrine mentioned as such. It is, however, implied (see John 14:15, 16 and 26; Matthew 28:19; 2 Corinthians 1:21, 22; 13:13; 1 Peter 1:2; Jude 20, 21). These verses reflect the worshiping life of the early church. Christians then as now knew that it is a mystery which cannot be explained, but it was their way of acknowledging the ways in which God was disclosed to them and experienced by them. God is too small if our acquaintance with him is limited to creation and providence, or if our Christain way of living is restricted to "following Jesus," or if our spiritual experience is "dated" because it does not receive daily renewal of the Spirit, wrote British Methodist G. Leslie Holdsworth. We need a great God, a "whole" God. The late Dorothy Sayers, lay theologian and detective story writer, used a good analogy in her book *The Mind of the Maker.** A book may be considered as thought—the idea in the writer's mind; as written—the express image of the idea. There is also the book read—the power of its effect on the responsive mind. So the creative idea that sees the entire creation complete represents the Father. The creative energy that commits the idea to writing represents the Word made flesh. The creative power, the meaning of the work and the reader's inward response represent the indwelling Spirit.

A sermon outline may well follow the "society in the godhead": God—the Creator; God—the Redeemer; God—the Sanctifier.

* (New York: Harcourt, Brace & World, Inc., 1941).

## Does God know you?

TEXT: *"But now that you know God—or, should I say, now that God knows you . . ."* (*Galatians 4:9, T.E.V.*).

"What do you or what does anyone know about God, Henry?" asked a Yale classmate of the late President Henry Sloane Coffin of Union Theological Seminary, New York. They met each other in a railway station. The college friend learned that the minister was proceeding to a boys' school to preach "about God." Replied Dr. Coffin: "I may not know much about God, but what I do know is so important I want to share it with those boys." The Apostle Paul knew how essential is a person's knowledge of God, his character, his action and purpose manifested through Christ. ". . . I know whom I have trusted," he told Timothy, "and I am sure that he is able to keep safe until that Day what he has entrusted to me" (2 Timothy 1:12). But Paul had another insight: it is not just in knowing God that Christian experience issues in conviction and assurance. It is being known and loved by God. To know that God knows us, loves us, and cares for us is truly to be saved, renewed, empowered.

## Postscript

TEXT: (*Galatians 6:11–18, T.E.V.*).

Postscripts sometimes contain the most important part of a letter. A son writes one of his rare letters from college, describes his academic activity and some of his social and athletic life. After the signature, "Love to all, Bob" comes the real "curve" to his pitch: "P.S. Send money quick! I'm really broke."

Paul apparently dictated his letters to a secretary, called in the ancient world an amanuensis. In Galatians he takes the pen from the secretary and adds not only his signature but an eight-verse P.S. He has something very significant to say in conclusion. He writes in what someone today would call "bold capitals," what translators give as "huge letters." One New Testament translator, Dr. J. B. Phillips, is sure he meant, "Notice how heavily I underline these words to you." (Galatians 6:11, footnote, J.B.P.)

What is in this postscript and what does it mean to us as in these Lenten weeks we follow in imagination and faith Christ's pilgrimage to the cross whereon he was to die?

1) He gives solemn warning against those who insist religion must be legalistic, conform to certain external requirements. They are playing it safe to escape any persecution; in our generation, to escape meeting the resistance of those who oppose applying Christian standards and concern to actual situations.

2) He underscores the centrality of the Cross of Christ for us. The Cross and the Man who suffered and died on it are our boast. Somehow, Christ crucified is the power of God to becoming a new person, a new creation. Placarded against the skyline of our lives is the cross, symbol of a principle, the principle of dying to selfish claims and finding the "world" —the pagan culture—a dead and deadly thing to be transformed by God in Christ.

3) Paul proclaims this principle as the guide which will lead anyone into peace and compassion.

4) At the very end of the postscript this dauntless Christian flings a defiance at his enemies, the foes of Christ. "Let no one give me any more trouble;" he says, "for the scars I have on my body show that I am the slave of Jesus" (verse 17). It is as if Paul is saying, "Don't let anyone waste his time or energy trying to stop or attack me. My scars are proof that I am Christ's servant—I bear his marks—and I am immune from harm." Of course they could lash him and imprison him and kill him, but they could not reach or destroy the real person. Then he reverts quickly to the gentleness of a Christian and prays that the wonderful kindness, the invincible goodness of Christ, may be with their spirits.

## What God has done for Christians

TEXT: *"Let us give thanks to the God and Father of our Lord Jesus Christ! For he has blessed us, in our union with Christ, by giving us every spiritual gift in the heavenly world. Before the world was made, God had already chosen us to be his in Christ, so that we would be holy and without fault before him. Because of his love . . ." (Ephesians 1:3, 4, T.E.V.).*

*And so it was with you also: when you heard the true message, the Good News that brought you salvation, you believed in Christ, and God put his stamp of ownership on you by giving you the Holy Spirit he had promised. The Spirit is the guarantee that we shall receive what God has promised his people, and assures us that God will give complete freedom to those who are his. Let us praise his glory!"* (*verses 13, 14*).

1) Paul has really "hit the jet stream" and is "revved up" as he attempts to describe God's grand design and what God has done for Christians. In the Greek in which he wrote, the entire passage from verse 3 to verse 14 is one single sentence! Calvinists delighted in this section because in it they found support for their doctrines of predestination and election. We must remember that Paul was speaking as "a man in Christ," not as a systematic theologian. He did believe that God chooses us to be his saved and responsible sons and daughters. When you experience God's grace you know that it is no accident; God took the initiative. It is all amazing.

2) Consider what God has done for Christians. Such consideration induces not pride but gratitude. (a) God has chosen us. Recall Jesus' saying to his first followers in John 15:16. Somehow, as Luther said, in spite of ourselves we are led like an old blind horse into the road of trust, obedience, service. (b) Think of the staggering generosity of God's choice. ". . . every spiritual gift in the heavenly world" is better translated as J. B. Phillips has done it, "every possible spiritual benefit as citizens of Heaven!" "Heaven" means the spiritual world which is not "out there" or "over there" but here, lying about us in infancy, youth, every age. Some things we can acquire by hard work, by skill, by what we call native endowment. But not the deep security which God gives; not "peace at the center"; not all that Paul means by being "in Christ." (c) God's reason for choosing us is that we might be "holy and blameless children living within his constant care." "Holy and blameless" seems, as the English say, "a bit much." We shall never be that perfect this side of resurrection. The words translated "holy and blameless" mean "different" and that which may be a worthy offering to God. Christians are called to be far above the average and ahead of their pagan or respectable contemporaries. Christians are more than just decent,

respectable people. We are never to be satisfied but always to concentrate on offering the best (see Romans 12:1). (d) Consider what God has prepared for us: "And here is the staggering thing—that in all which will one day belong to him we have been promised a share." This is no stock promotion, no prospectus for a heavenly investment trust; it is the kind of God with whom we have to do. "Consider what God has done" and respond.

## Father and the family

TEXT: *"For this reason, then, I fall on my knees before the Father, from whom every family in heaven and on earth receives its true name"* (*Ephesians 3:14, 15, T.E.V.*).

Paul is saying, "For this reason, seeing the greatness of this plan by which you are built together in Christ, I kneel in prayer to the Father, from whom all fatherhood takes its title and derives its name, its nature." On Mother's Day we celebrate not merely the significance of mother's role, but of father and mother and children, for May's second Sunday is National Family Week's culmination. Mother herself undoubtedly will vote for this expansion of the tribute; she must have been embarrassed by panegyrics of praise of her idealized "image."

1) What is happening to the family in the Western world is a question educators, Christian sociologists as well as non-Christian sociologists, and concerned persons of every type are asking. Answers vary. Certainly the "new morality," the affluent society, the highly mobile way of living, the ignorance of or indifference to what we call spiritual values all are factors in the changing pattern of the family. Nevertheless, with all the changes, most of us continue to regard the family as the basic unit of human community and are convinced that, like the individual, the family must be strengthened by finding "strength and power through God's Spirit in (our) inner being," if it is to fulfill its role in God's design.

2) Cliché it may be, but there is more than a smidgeon of truth in the slogan, "The family that prays together stays together." If it is impossible to use a modern form of family worship in the home, the family may and should worship

together in God's house, not only on Mother's Day or Family Sunday, but on every Lord's Day. The prayer that teaches us to pray, which Jesus gave us, is the prayer of the family: "This is the way you should pray: 'Our Father, . . .'" To know God in Jesus Christ is to realize that the "ground of being" is much more than Thomas Hardy's "dreaming, dark, dumb Thing / That turns the handle of the idle Show." The deep meaning of "Abba, father" (Mark 14:36; Romans 8:15; Galatians 4:6) tells us that God is indeed fatherlike and therefore cares for each of his children. This caring (Christlike love) is undeserved, all-inclusive, practical. To pray together to our Father is to have our relationship to God settled and established. It also strengthens the bonds of the family, without attempting to put members of the family into a straightjacket of forced piety and repressive rules.

3) God our Father, known and experienced through trusting faith in Jesus Christ, hallows the human family that unites in loving response to him. A second fact must be stressed: father, mother, and child in the human family must know that when they say "*Our Father* . . ." the whole family of mankind is included. The use of the word "our" in our address to God, in our thought of God, "ends all exclusiveness." Wrote a New Testament scholar recently: "If God is *our* Father, then our fellow man is our brother. The only possible basis for democracy is the conviction of the fatherhood of God. The only value that man possesses as man is that he is the child of God. Nationalism, racialism, snobbery, class distinctions, the color bar, apartheid stand uncompromisingly condemned in the two words which open the Lord's Prayer." No one need fear what is happening to the family whose own family is centered down in the God and Father of the Lord Jesus Christ. (Note: an illustration of God's love of the least, lowest, and presumed lost is given by Dr. Paul Tournier).* A young patient's trouble stemmed partially at least from overhearing her father say regarding herself, as the youngest of a large family: "We could well have done without that one!" God could never say that of any of his human children. Also, to picture the detailed care of God, there is the insight of the late Professor J. E. McFadyen. He believed that when you put Jesus' saying about the sparrow falling to the ground (Matthew 10:29) back into

* *Op. cit.*, Paul Tournier, p. 146.

the Aramaic it could read that when a sparrow *lights* on the ground, hops on the ground, God sees it and knows.

## Whose church is it?

TEXT: "*. . . Christ is himself the Savior of the church, his body. . . .*" (*Ephesians* 5:23, T.E.V.).

"*. . . Christ loved the church and gave his life for it. He did this to dedicate the church to God, by his word, after making it clean by the washing in water, in order to present the church to himself, in all its beauty, pure and faultless, without spot or wrinkle, or any other imperfection*" (*verses* 25–27).

A brother pastor, James Stuart Dickson of Alexandria, Virginia, asked a congregation recently, "Whose church is this?" Who hasn't heard the unfortunate remark that such-and-such a church is a company church, or Vincent Moneybag's church, or the church that belongs to a certain clique? Our Florida preacher acknowledged the partial truth of frequently heard answers to the question.

1) "It is Dr. (or the Reverend Mr.) Blank's church." Inevitably, in Protestant circles, the preacher of the Word, if effective or popular or widely known, has his name attached to the actual building in which he preaches. For purposes of identification this may not be wholly reprehensible, but it can be unfortunate because no living household of God belongs to any man.

2) Then the church is a Baptist, or a Lutheran, or a Methodist, or a Presbyterian, or a United, or an Anglican or some other denomination's church. In some communions the local church may be legally the property of the communion. This is an honest designation, but it is not a complete one. For to be a living church within the "Great Church" every church must be Christ's own church. Christ purchased the church with his own blood. "He did this to dedicate the church to God . . ." said the writer of the Ephesian letter in our New Testament.

What makes a church truly Christian? How can we help?

## How outgoing can you get?

TEXT: (*Philippians 2:5–11, T.E.V.*).

Introduction. An "outgoing" person is praised by us as our predecessors praised the equivalent, a selfless soul. Prudently, however, we set limits on "outgoingness"; you must not give yourself, your energies, time, and money so completely to others, or to a good cause, that you yourself suffer. This is the difference between Christ and us. In the passage selected as the epistle for Palm Sunday in most lectionaries, Christ gives himself for us so utterly, and gives up prerogatives and the greatest prize (equality with God), that he is too great for us to understand, and too much for many to accept as God-in-a-human-life, our Lord and Savior. Biblical scholars (see *Interpreter's Bible,** also William Barclay's Study Bible†) assert that Philippians 2:5–11 is in many ways the greatest, most moving passage that Paul ever wrote.

1) Paul moves into orbit around God's tremendous self-giving in Christ after the Apostle had been bogged down in party wrangling and the un-Christian spiritual pride of the congregation at Philippi. This true pastor who just a moment before confessed that he sometimes wished that he were dead for the sake of closer communion with Christ makes a noble appeal for unity and harmony. Keep Jesus Christ steadily in sight is his directive counseling. Christ "went all out" not only to make himself a man, but to make himself the servant, the kind of servant—literally a slave—of whom Isaiah had spoken. He lived and died in perfect obedience to God. He divested himself of all divine glory to endure the final humiliation of the cross.

2) How outgoing can God get? The answer is given as we let this picture in Philippians 2 speak to us. The answer is given in that broken yet majestic man on the cross. Love is not only, as the sentimental ballad declares, "the sweet mystery of life," it is the incredibly shattering and transforming power of God for salvation. Americans do not like to be servants. Understandably, we hate being slaves. But it is to this kind

* (Nashville: Abingdon Press, 1955), vol. II, p. 46.

† *Letters to the Philippians, Colossians and Thessalonians* (Philadelphia: The Westminster Press, 1959).

of servant life and slavery that we are called by the One who is our supreme example. In the famous inner-city Church of St. Martin's-in-the-Fields, London, England, someone reported reading this definition of a Christian: "A Christian is a mind through which Christ thinks; a heart through which Christ loves; a voice through which Christ speaks; a hand through which Christ helps." Whoever framed that definition knew that Christ "made himself nothing, assuming the nature of a slave . . . humbled himself, and in obedience accepted even death—death on a cross" (Philippians 2:7, 8, N.E.B.). How outgoing can we get? As outgoing as Jesus Christ himself, and "out of your life in Christ Jesus" (verse 5).

3) It was for this perfect obedience and humility that this "Man for others" is now supreme, exalted above the whole universe. What Isaiah attributed to God, Paul attributes to Christ (Isaiah 45:23). This is what the New Testament means by "Lord." This is why all must bow before him, not simply in outward gesture or posture, but in obedient service. It is because Christ is the servant of all that we may speak as our fathers did of "the crown rights of the Redeemer."

## Keep going

TEXT: ". . . *I keep going on to possess it, for Christ Jesus has already possessed me. Of course, brothers, I really do not think that I have already reached it; the one thing I do, however, is to forget what is behind me and do my best to reach what is ahead. So I run straight toward the goal in order to win the prize, which is God's call through Christ Jesus to the life above*" (*Philippians 3:12–14, T.E.V.*).

"I keep going." This is a word we need when summer slackness (or sickness in our body politic) begins to diminish.

1) More important, "keep going" is a word of God to young people in high school, college, military service, or some other form of work. Keep going toward a worthy and well-defined goal. What if you cannot see or choose a goal? Ask yourself, where do I want to be ten years from now? Youth need not be deterred nor diverted because of its youth. "Let no man despise your youth," was St. Paul's wise counsel for

his younger colleague Timothy. How one would like to say to academic and vocational and spiritual dropouts, "Keep going, not only to realize your own potential, but because you may have a part in fulfilling God's design for his human family."

In May 1968 when student protest disrupted college and university administrations, a *Life* magazine essay writer suggested among many reasons for the student rebellion was that today's undergraduates "are apt to be bright but dreamy . . . from families that are prosperous, politically active and liberal." After observing that they showed (Dr.) Spock marks from their upbringing, the writer said, "They have less direction than previous generations." But when a person of any age gains a sense of direction he needs perseverance, the kind the Apostle voiced when he said, honestly and doggedly, "I keep going." Said a headmistress of a once-famous girls' school to her students, "Walk with dignity and finish strong." Keep going!

2) This is a word for those who are growing older. Note that the phrase is not "getting old." When a woman member of a church complained that one of the pastors was "just too young," a venerable elder sagely replied: "Well, that is a condition which is bound to improve at the rate of twenty-four hours a day." Christians can keep growing intellectually, spiritually and emotionally as they grow older. Who was it said that "life really begins, not when we are forty or sixty-five or any age; life begins when we become working partners of Jesus Christ"? With Christ, age and aging lose their power to throw us. As John Bodo once wrote: "You are as old as you are Christian—and as young." Keep going!

3) Keep going, urges the Lord of life, toward wholeness, Christlikeness, and a more Christian, free and responsible society. Christ came to give all God's children abundant life, and he set no limits in terms of time, heredity or past achievement record. Keep running, says a great scripture: Hebrews 12:1, 2. As Prince Philip remarked in an address, "You only live to regret the times you have given up." These may seem to be the worst of times. Who knows? Our successors may look back at us and envy us the challenges of living in a volcanic, creative generation when humanity struck its tents and marched toward Christian goals. Without violence or fear or hatred, without despair or unrealistic optimism, Christ bids his church keep going toward a more Christian order.

There are times when we need to relax, to be casual, to saunter. We cannot always be like an archer's bow, taut and tense. Is this not a time when we need to respond to Philip Doddridge's robust and atheltic words: "Awake, my soul, stretch every nerve, And press with vigor on"? One preacher was sure that the great threat to the Christian life is not atheism or agnosticism or communism but somnambulism. Keep going!

## Formula for great living

TEXT: "*I . . . do my best to reach what is ahead*" (*Philippians 3:13, T.E.V.*).

"*We love because God first loved us*" (*1 John 4:19*).

"*. . . an apostle of Christ Jesus . . . our hope*" (*1 Timothy 1:1*).

1) Is there a formula for great living? For living with what a former Harvard University president called "the durable satisfactions of life"? Rightly most mature people suspect anyone who offers a simplistic (or oversimplified) prescription for life, liberty, and happiness. Biblical Christianity is no "science of mind" through which, if you discover and practice its basic principles, you will gain more money, enjoy a happier love life, escape the conflicts and confusions of the secular city. Years ago a British theologian, Professor P. Carnegie Simpson, write a book entitled *Essentials.** He was sure, as a Christian and as a Christian philosopher, that these are basically two: something to do, and someone to love. Recently Immanuel Kant, the famed eighteenth-century philosopher, was credited with a threefold recipe for happiness. Interpreted Christianly it is more complete—at least more specific than Dr. Simpson's basic ingredients of a successful life pattern: (1) Something to do. Even in a world where workdays will be greatly reduced due to the technological revolution, we shall all need something significant to do. (2) Someone to love. (I would add "and someone who loves us whose love we are able to receive.") (3) Something to hope for. We have to have

* (Peterborough: The R. R. Smith Co., Inc., 1930).

a star to sail by in a dark night. Christ as God's self-disclosure and self-giving provides these essentials.

## Man alive—in the shadows

TEXT: (*Colossians 1:11–15, 18, T.E.V.*). (*See also John 20:11, 13–16.*)

If you had been faking the story of Jesus' resurrection you would not have written about it in the way the gospel writers did. You would do it more dramatically, more consistently, and with something of the "TV spectacular" touch. But the narratives all show us the man Jesus alive after death, and alive through the shadows of doubt, despair, bereavement chilling his most intimate followers' souls. But now, nearly 2,000 years later, it seems to many a bit of the stuff of which dreams are made. (a) But the risen Lord comes even in the shadows of doubt and unbelief. Paul states the matter bluntly (1 Corinthians 15:17). No resurrection of Christ, no Christian faith; no living Lord, no living church. Today the Lord points to his body the church, with all its inadequacies and self-inflicted wounds, and says, as to skeptical Thomas, "Put your finger here . . . stop your doubting and believe!" (John 20:27). (b) The Risen Lord enters into the shadows and darkness made by our moral failures, by our sin. Our sins are forgiven. We can be free. This acceptance and pardon are not cheaply won. Resurrection now—for us! "He has delivered us from the dominion of darkness and transferred us to the kingdom of his beloved Son, in whom we have redemption, the forgiveness of sins." (c) God enters into the shadows of death to lead us through the darkest valley of all into his marvelous light of life eternal. Look again at Colossians, chapter 1. "He is the head of his body, the church; he is the source of the body's life; he is the first-born Son who was raised from death, in order that he alone might have the first place in all things. For it was by God's own decision that the Son has in himself the full nature of God" (Colossians 1:18–20).

Death is an enemy, but it will be destroyed. This is why Easter is full of pipe organs, trumpets, alleluias, hosannas, cheers! God has banished the shadows of death's power.

## Your secret—and God's

TEXT: (*Colossians 1:24–29, T.E.V.*).

Introduction: Secrets fascinate human beings. Consider the appeal of the TV program, "I've Got a Secret"; the appeal of gossip, to discover a secret about persons; "beauty secrets," "secret recipes."

Dr. Paul Tournier, Swiss Christian thinker and psychiatrist, in his recent book, *Secrets,** makes a convincing case for three stages in the growth of an individual into a real person. (1) A child needs to have secrets from parents and other adults, to discover himself and to escape parental domination. (2) A child and a grown person need to be able to confide secrets to a chosen, trustworthy confidant. (3) A person needs to confide his secrets—burdens, doubts, fears, sins, hopes—to God. God knows the secrets of all hearts (see Psalm 139:1, 7:11, and 32:3, 5), and yet God asks us to share our secrets with him. Says Dr. Tournier: "God is waiting for us to choose him as confidant, because he, first, chose man as confidant." Says the Bible, God speaks through prophets and other responsive agents, and most clearly and transformingly in Jesus Christ. This dialogue with God is the means by which we become a mature person, mature "in Christ." Such dialogue is possible on a personal level in secrecy. Jesus said we must go into a secret place to hear God's whisper within our souls (Matthew 6:6). (4) God's secret is an "open secret." For us today it is what it was to the members of the First Church of Colossae. " . . . the secret is this: Christ is in you, which means that you will share the glory of God" (Colossians 1:27).

## What Christ nailed down on his cross

TEXT: (*Colossians 2:13, 14, T.E.V.*).

Truth reveals itself to the person who approaches mystery without prejudice. Long ago, Margaret Slattery, a once-prominent Christian laywoman, made that comment in a classroom. It has truth but not all the truth. When we ap-

* (Richmond: John Knox Press, 1965).

proach the mystery of what was done for us in and through the death of Jesus Christ we need to approach it with more than an open mind. Openness of course, but reverence and love also are required.

The Apostle Paul tries to explain the mystery of Christ's sacrifice. He uses one metaphor and then another. In this passage from Colossians he refers to an ancient practice. A debt could be canceled by nailing the document which proved the debt's existence on some conspicuous object in some public place. So, Paul suggests, by his death the Lord Jesus somehow cancels all our liabilities. We are forgiven by God himself. This is guaranteed by God's own writing on the cross.

We may not follow Paul here, but we can understand that some facts, some realities are "nailed down." (1) One is the reality of our sin, of all mankind's sin. We may prefer the word "failure." The cross shows what Professor John Knox called "the abominable depths of evil." (2) The cross of Christ nails down the amazing love and grace of God which goes to the limit to forgive us. Of course there is always forgiveness with God, but somehow the cross makes it real, if only because on the cross we realize how much pardon costs. (3) The cross nails down the truth that God must win. "He must reign." Christ died, yea, rather, rose again from the dead, and dieth no more. With the God we know in Jesus Christ, in his life, in his death, in his victory, what should be at last shall be.

## Brotherly love is something you do

TEXT: (*1 Thessalonians 4:9–12, T.E.V.*).

Love is something you do, says more than one teacher of ethics both Christian and secular. Brotherhood Week is still celebrated in the nation, but brotherly love of the quality advocated and described in the New Testament needs demonstration every week and every day. Here, in one of the earliest pieces of Christian writing we possess, Paul may be referring to a letter which his younger colleague Timothy brought back from Thessalonica. Of course, in writing advice to the Thessalonian Christians at the beginning, Paul writes as a true pastor, with love and encouragement. He recognized rightly that one of the heartening features of the church in that Greek city was their brotherly love. The word translated "brotherly love" is a word always used in the New Testament for it—*philadelphia.*

"The early Christian Churches were little companies of people where love was at a high temperature . . . Men were drawn to them irresistibly by the desire to share this life of love" (*Expositor's Bible*).* Could this be said of present-day churches? If it could be said, we would have no anxiety about the future of institutional Christianity; the renewal of present-day church structures would be continuous.

(1) This love was not limited to their own church: "you are in fact practising this rule of love towards all your fellow-Christians throughout Macedonia." Throughout the whole Roman province were individual Christians and Christian families as well as the two other churches. Paul had experienced the hospitality of the others. He urges the church members to "do better still." This is love, Christlike love, in action. "Do better still," says their father in God.

(2) They are to be ambitious not to be ambitious in the noisy, worldly sense. "Let it be your ambition to keep calm and look after your own business." Is this a bit of counsel inspired by the excited Christians who were sure that Christ's visible second coming to earth was near? Perhaps. It is good counsel for all Christians. Our brothers and sisters of the Religious Society of Friends have demonstrated the necessity of "peace at the center." Only so can we adequately engage in our spiritual warfare for God's kingdom. "Endeavor to live quietly," is James Moffatt's translation. "Attend to your own business." Christians may become so absorbed in extraneous matters, so immersed in good causes beyond their homes and communities that they neglect their homework. It need not be "either/or," but if we do not do our homework it is unlikely we shall be equipped for Christ's peace corps in other areas.

(3) Then comes this practical directive: "work with your hands." Paul was not thinking of manual work as a kind of therapy, although many have found it to be healing. "Attend to your own business" is a cure all of us busybodies need. Working with our hands is a duty. By this is meant: do the work that is yours as Christ would do it if he were in your place,

* *Expositor's Bible,* edited by W. R. Nicholl (London: Hodder and Stoughton, 1888).

with fidelity, with honesty, with consideration for others, and with the joy of knowing it may help advance the great cause of God's justice, peace, and brotherhood.

Worth retelling is the New England story of a day when sudden darkness enveloped a section of the earth at a time when there was frenzied expectancy of the end of the world. Someone in the legislative assembly cried fearfully, "It is the coming of Christ. It is the end of the world!" The old presiding officer ordered lights to be produced. "Bring in candles," he said, "and get on with your work. If the Lord is coming, how better can he find us than quietly doing our duty?"

## Sound reasons for gratitude

TEXT: "*We must thank God at all times for you, brothers! It is right for us to do so, because your faith is growing so much and the love each of you has for the others is becoming greater*" (*2 Thessalonians 1:3, T.E.V.*).

"Did I tell you how wonderful I think you are?" was the way a brave and gracious woman ended her letters to members of her family to whom she wrote during the stormy, tragic years of the American Civil War. Paul says this to the Thessalonian Christians in his second letter. They are indeed brothers in Christ, and he is thankful to God for them. Why? Because (1) their faith is growing, and growing so much. Faith is not static when it is placed in the dynamic God whom the apostle knew from first-hand experience. A once-prominent preacher, the late John Henry Jowett, wrote during his own final illness to a dear friend who was also moving on the last mile of his earthly journey, "Remember that Jesus Christ is infinitely greater than the best things we have ever said about Him." He is like His action, exceeding abundantly above all that we ask or think. Therefore, our faith must grow as we discern His greatness in creation and in His redemptive power. (2) The second sound reason for thanking God for his fellow Christians is one which should stimulate our gratitude for companions in Christ's service: "because . . . the love each of you has for the others is becoming greater." Dr. Howard Thurman once said of Christ's love for the lowest and the least, even for Mary of Magdala: "He loved her into newness of life." Christlike love, uniting all other kinds, does work the miracle.

"See how these Christians love one another!" was first of all a sincere tribute of non-Christian observers. Sometimes it is said sarcastically when outsiders observe the wrangling and backbiting of Church members. Growing faith and increasing love are the authentic marks of the living church of our Lord Jesus Christ. In the last chapter of this brief letter the Apostle urges us not to yield to fatigue in our service of Christ: "But you, brothers, must not get tired of doing good" (3:13).

## Words you may trust

TEXT: *"This is a true saying, to be completely accepted and believed"* (*1 Timothy 4:9, T.E.V.*).

What words did Paul mean? The words that preceded this statement or the words that follow? Scholars incline to believe that it refers to the words that go before: ". . . spiritual exercise is valuable in every way" (verse 8).

So many words spoken by others prove untrustworthy. If these are the words we can trust, all shall yet be well. We can take whatever comes. Toil and trouble, crises and crosses we can endure if ultimate deliverance is sure. (1) The Christian way is not an easy way, and anyone who says it is, is wrong. (2) The goal of the Christian way is God. He is our journey's end as well as our present guide, guard, and strength. (3) The Christian is the person who has hope, realistic and enduring. Why? Because the Christian hopes in God. "It is because he sees God at his journey's end, it is because life is lived in the presence of God and ends in His still nearer presence, that the Christian is willing to endure as he does" (William Barclay's commentary on this passage in *The Study Bible*).

On a summer morning in 1951, one of America's truly Christian prophets died when Dr. Ernest Fremont Tittle, of First Methodist Church, Evanston, Illinois, slumped forward on his desk and entered completely the life eternal. He had been a prophet in the Christian sense, an enemy of all social, national, and international evils. He was maligned as a Communist and wild radical. He spoke unpalatable truth in love. Only three days before he died he had stood in the pulpit he made famous and preached on "Hope." Listen to his closing words in the last sermon he preached:

"Blessed is the man who repents of his sins and seeks

the forgiveness of God; for he shall have hope. Blessed is the man who dedicates himself to God and his purpose of good in the world; for he shall have hope. Blessed are they who trusting in God come to know from personal experience that in everything God works with those who love him to bring about what is good. Blessed are they; for they, even in the darkest hour, shall have hope." To us, the words Paul wrote to Roman Christians are not only a benediction but an urgent invitation (see Romans 15:13).

## Formula for victory

TEXT: (*1 Timothy 6:11, 12, T.E.V.*).

1) Who would not give much to discover or devise a formula for victory over war, over racial hatred and injustice, over the sins which trip us up so frequently and make havoc of what God must intend to be a life of harmony and creative quality?

Someone called attention to such a formula in the first letter of the Apostle Paul to Timothy. In the older translation of the King James Version you have a triple directive. In the familiar translation each directive is a verb beginning with the same letter. Here is the triple directive, the formula for Christian victory: (1) *Flee* those subtle enemies of integrity and usefulness which he lists in the preceding verses. It is more than the folk wisdom of "he who fights and runs away will live to fight another day." In this world of conflict, of challenge and response, there are some things to avoid. There is virtue as well as power in some negative thinking! But "No" is not the only or the chief response of Christ's man or woman. (2) "*Fight* the good fight of faith" (verse 12), urges the great soldier of Christ. To fight is to strive, to struggle. We are not carried to heaven here and now or hereafter on what the old hymn writer called "flowery beds of ease." "You can't get to heaven in a rocking chair," in a jet plane, or in a noise-free automobile. "This do and thou shalt live," said our Lord. (3) In the verses written to Timothy the third part of the formula comes second. It seems to one preacher that logically it should come third. "*Follow* after righteousness, godliness, faith, love, patience, meekness" (verse 11).

Surely spelling out these virtues, these qualities of the

good life, is one way of answering the question, What does it mean to follow Christ in today's wild but not hopeless world? Flee, fight, follow. Who would not obey who heard Christ call?

## Letter to the saints in . . .

TEXT: *"Keep the good things that have been entrusted to you, through the power of the Holy Spirit who lives in us"* (*2 Timothy 1:14, T.E.V.*).

"Keep the great securities of your faith intact, by aid of the Holy Spirit that dwells within us" (Moffatt).

This sermon may use the form of a letter to the saints in your particular community. Paul would begin such an epistle, "To the saints who live in Podunk . . ." (or whatever the community's name may be). To New Testament writers a saint was far from perfect or complete, as even quick reading of the New Testament epistles makes clear. The saints are God's people, Christians, human beings who are sinners but forgiven sinners, and who (as the Wesleys would say) are on the way to perfection.

What are "the great securities of the faith"?

1) Primary and basic is a growing, vital faith (believing trust) in the living God whom Jesus Christ disclosed and brings near. God may be dead for some who still wish to retain Jesus Christ at least as a stance and symbol, an ethic and way of living. But Paul would be dumbfounded if you said you could be a "Christian atheist." If God ever lived, he is alive now and forever. He that will confide himself to the God who is in Christ will know. He that starts doing his will as this may be discerned through scripture, through study of the needs to be met, and through spiritual companionship with Christ—he will know. This God of holy, righteous love is the ground of all being and the guide and guardian of all who bet their lives on him.

2) Another great security is bound up with the first: the supremacy of Christ. Read even a little of Dietrich Bonhoeffer's lectures, *Christ the Center*,* and you will find insight to sharpen your own as you let your Christology show through. He is indeed "the man for others," and he is more: God-in-a-human-life as no other has been; Savior, Lord, companion of our inner lives on every road we take.

* (New York: Harper & Row, Publishers, 1966), pp. 9–118.

3) Christlike love is one of the "great securities" of the Christian faith. To trust in God as completely as may be possible and to love our fellow humans unconditionally is to be an instrument of Christ's spirit and therefore of his invincible love. This means that we love our enemies, which is impossible if we do not have that extra incentive and power the scripture calls "grace."

4) Another security of the faith, another abiding value which we are to keep, is our commitment to Christ's program. To be committed to Christ is to be committed to what he called God's kingdom. The fatherly rule of God in every relationship, in every area of human existence, is one of the essentials. Solitary or private religion is not to be found in the Bible—at least not found with any approval. God's dealings are chiefly with a people, a redeemed and redemptive community. Christian discipleship is personal, of course, but the person is within social context, and to be "in Christ" is to be involved with this corrupt yet potentially good and great world here and now. The church must never be a ghetto, and therefore must be a base of operations, a supply center from which Christ's troops go forth to engage in their moral and spiritual warfare with the enemies of God's justice and love.

5) You will think of other "securities of your faith"—the church itself, the Holy Spirit, worship and the Bible. Who can keep such securities intact? No one, no group, no congregation, as such, as Paul makes clear. "Keep the great securities of your faith intact, by aid of the Holy Spirit that dwells within us." We are not alone. We need not strive and strain to keep alive and relevant to the essentials of the gospel: the Holy Spirit has been given us. This power and grace live within us. As an old-fashioned saint once said, "We can change the gospel hymn, 'I need Thee every hour' to 'I *have* Thee every hour.'" You may end your "letter" with a Christian signature: "Your brother in Christ." Better yet, "Affectionately your brother (or sister) in Christ. . . ."

## Christians—tough or tender?

TEXT: (*2 Timothy 2:23–25, T.E.V.*).

Christians, and churchmen generally, are said to be too easy, too flaccid, too tender with the majority of their fellow members. Says more than one serious Christian, "The church ought to get tough with its apathetic, timid, or noninvolved members." The "establishment," that is, the organized church, will never be the servant church unless its members accept discipline.

One suggestion is that dues be levied on members, that every one of us be assessed what an informed committee may decide we could pay. Moreover, we should end any tendency of the local church to be a pleasant, ingrown ghetto for its members. We must move from worship to "where the action is" on behalf of ending poverty, social injustice of every kind, racial discrimination, and international war. In words reminiscent of the Navy, Christians on church rolls must "shape up or ship out." Contribute sacrificially or resign. We have sympathy with such strictures and suggestions. Here is an elder statesman of the early church saying to a young colleague, "Yes, 'reprove, rebuke, exhort.' Let them have it; tell it as it is." But then Paul adds, ". . . encourage, using the utmost patience in your teaching (2 Timothy 4:2, J.B.P.).

1) Christians, like children in school, are at differing stages of development. We are in various grades. We can never have truth or knowledge or skill pounded into us.

2) Skill in personal relationships—and certainly in personal relationships of Christians—requires plain speaking on occasion, but always, as the Apostle says elsewhere, we are to "speak the truth in love." Is there any other way to get the truth through to another? Auto body repairmen remove a bulge from a piece of metal, such as a dented fender, not by mighty blows on the bulge, but often by hammering gently some distance from the bulge. It is then that the bulge gradually disappears.

3) Personal and social evangelism requires patience and gentleness, neither of which are incompatible with direct, honest analysis and plain speaking. "Our impulse," writes a wise Christian leader, "is to take them by the spiritual scruff of the neck and shake them into believing!" Our Lord put this temptation behind him, and he was said to have possessed the strength that men call weakness. "The Lord's servant must not quarrel. He must be kind toward all, a good and patient teacher, who is gentle as he corrects his opponents" (verses 24, 25). Thank God he gives grace for such control and strategy!

## All change here

TEXT: "*It may be that God will give them the opportunity to repent and come to know the truth. And then they will return to their senses and escape from the trap of the Devil . . .*" (2 *Timothy* 2:25, 26, *T.E.V.*).

1) When did you last hear a sermon on conversion? It is a term used more frequently in banks (as is redemption!) or in the technical discussions of psychologists and psychiatrists. Christianity is a religion of redemption. No one is ever saved from anything or saved to anything without what our fathers meant by "conversion." The third chapter of John was a favorite section of scripture for those who had, as the old phrase put it, "a passion for souls." Today the word, the act, the scripture may be more favored by those we call "hot gospelers" than by the average Protestant churchman.

2) Conversion in its true meaning is what Christ came to achieve. The Apostle Paul writing to Timothy advises him how to handle refractory persons. He bids him be a good teacher, tolerant and gentle when discipline is needed. He also reminds him that "the Lord may grant them a change of heart and show them the truth." When that happens conversion has taken place in the religious meaning of the word.

An unknown Christian said that there are three conversions in a Christian's life: "First to Christ, then to the church, and then back to the world." (1) We change our "hearts," minds, and emotions, concerning Jesus Christ. We give all that we know of ourselves to all that we know of God in Jesus Christ (Archbishop William Temple's phrasing when appealing to students to make up their minds and change their way of living). (2) We are converted to the church. Solitary, private religion is inadequate and sub-Christian. It is in the fellowship of Christians that we become more Christian. The church is integral to Christian faith. "Where two or three are gathered" in Christ's name—"in Christ"—there Christ is present and operative. (3) Our third conversion, or the third element in a truly Christian change of mind and life, is to the world. We are to accept "Christian worldliness" and practice it. We are, as the Salvation Army used to say, "saved to serve" in our society and culture; to be responsible, socially aware Christians. We are changed by God's spirit in order to work with God to change the world of war into a world of peace, to change the world of injustice and cruelty into a world more just and compassionate.

## All Christians have a priest

TEXT: *"Let us, then, hold firmly to the faith we profess. For we have a great high priest who has gone into the very presence of God—Jesus, the Son of God"* (*Hebrews 4:14, T.E.V.*).

This is an Ascension Day theme. The event and its derivative doctrine are neglected by most churchmen outside the "prayer book" communions. Ascension Day need not fall on a Sunday, but it may well be observed in prayers, hymns and in sermon on the Sunday preceding the fixed date of May 27.

Introduction may acknowledge that the Ascension of our Lord sounds prescientific, irrelevant and obscure to the average Christian. The space age has increased the difficulties. Heaven is not "up there." Space is up there, and space is neither up nor down! Bishop J. A. T. Robinson's *Honest to God* has a point, even though the point was made by many Christian thinkers before his book appeared. Years ago the late Dr. Joseph Fort Newton prayed, "Our Father who art in heaven, on earth, everywhere. . . ." If anyone is troubled about where Jesus ascended following his resurrection, help may be found in British Methodist W. Russell Maltby's words: Jesus "went out of there into the everywhere, out of some men's sight that he might be near all men's hearts." * Nevertheless the relevant truth of the Ascension is more than the truth that because of his Ascension Christ is present everywhere. Christ is not merely a universal presence sharing the authority of God the Father. He is at work in the world for which he died and rose again. This work will never be complete until he conquers all enemies of God's fatherly rule and delivers the kingdom to the Father (1 Corinthians 15:24–26).

What is the present work or operation of the Risen and Ascended Lord? He is our great high priest. As one said, Christ ascended is our access to God. He is nearer than we can dream,

* From a pamphlet, "The Meaning of the Resurrection" (London: The Epworth Press, n.d.).

not visible to our eyes but within sound of our prayers. Think of his threefold "office" or ministry.

1) Christ is our priest. He is qualified to represent us in the divine Presence. Think of the implications of the New English Bible translation of Hebrews 7:26: "Such a high priest does indeed fit our condition—devout, guileless, undefiled, separated from sinners, raised high above the heavens." (a) His humanity is our hope: "For ours is not a high priest unable to sympathize with our weaknesses, but one who, because of his likeness to us, has been tested every way, only without sin" (Hebrews 4:15, N.E.B.). (b) His intimate relationship to God: "Thou art my Son." (c) His appointment by God: ". . . it was granted by God, who said to him, 'Thou art my Son . . .' " (verse 5, N.E.B.). See also Hebrews 5:6, 10.

2) The Ascended Christ is our Mediator, "the Man-in-the-Middle." Hebrews 7:25 (N.E.B.): ". . . he remains for ever. That is why he is also able to save absolutely those who approach God through him; he is always living to plead on their behalf." Only this Man on our side can bring us back to God when we have rebeled against him through our egotistical pride, our alienation from our brother man, our attempt to usurp God's place.

3) The Ascended Lord is the Intercessor. Again the affirmation of Hebrews 7:25 (N.E.B.): ". . . he is always living to plead on their behalf." Prayer is not our activity alone. As St. Paul wrote to the Christians in Rome: ". . . the Spirit comes to the aid of our weakness. We do not even know how we ought to pray, but through our inarticulate groans the Spirit himself is pleading for us, and God who searches our inmost being knows what the Spirit means, because he pleads for God's own people in God's own way . . ." (Romans 8:26, 27, N.E.B.). (Sermons should be enriched by the preacher's study of New Testament teaching about Christ's priesthood. In addition to Hebrews see John 17, John 14:6, Romans 5:2, Ephesians 2:18, 3:12.)

Other sermon outlines may be related to Pentecost or Whitsunday. "Christianity on Two Levels" might be the title of a sermon dealing with the gift of the Holy Spirit to life in the "soaring seventies" of this century. For the text choose Acts 19:2. (1) The ground floor: belief in God's reality as disclosed in the event of Jesus Christ. (2) The second floor is reached when we accept the gift of the Spirit. Supercharged with spiritual energy we are provided with (a) power to endure whatever comes and power to overcome; (b) power to be a Christian world citizen. Acts 10 and 15 show that the church's world mission followed Pentecost and that this meant a costly, pain-filled fellowship.

## Let's stir up our neighbors!

TEXT: *"Let us be concerned with one another, to help one another to show love and to do good"* (*Hebrews 10:24, T.E.V.*).

Let's stir up our neighbors! "Are you serious?" any church member might ask. What we want is less stirring up, whether by swinging teen-agers, juveniles practicing their musical instruments, or agitation to welcome minority group citizens into our neighborhood. The writer of the New Testament letter to Hebrew Christians, after pleading for faithful worship of God and for keeping a grip on what we believe (verses 19–23), asks us to do some thinking about how we may "help one another to show love and to do good." This is love's specialty: to think of one another's needs and possibilities and to encourage one another to love and active goodness (see also N.E.B., verse 24).

Then comes the directive which in every generation has left many good people and not a few Christians "cold." As we think how we may encourage one another to Christlike love and translate love into good deeds, *let us attend church regularly!* Nonattendance by Christians is no new phenomenon! Back in the days of the New Testament church some withdrew from the Christian fellowship and the public worship of God. Our New Testament writer is sure that this is a dangerous thing. As Dr. J. Harry Cotton put it in his exposition of the passage in the *Interpreter's Bible,* "Let a man break fellowship with the church and he is on his way to denying the faith." * J. B. Phillips translates it in these words, "Let us not hold aloof from our church meetings as some do."

Why go to church? Stephen F. Winward gives four cogent reasons in *A Modern ABeCeDary for Protestants.*†

* (Nashville: Abingdon Press, 1963), vol. 11, pp. 737–38.
† (New York: Association Press, 1964), pp. 104–5.

(1) *Go to church to meet God* (Matthew 18:20). Worship is keeping our appointment with the living God. (2) *Go to church to listen to God.* God speaks through the Scripture read and expounded, through the proclamation of Christ the Word "from the written word, by the spoken word." "Speak, Lord, for thy servant heareth" (1 Samuel 3:9, K.J.V.). (3) *Go to church to receive God.* As we open our lives to God's Spirit we receive through sermon and sacrament, prayer, and praise, his grace of forgiveness, direction, support, joy, and love (Isaiah 6:1–8). (4) *Go to church to give yourself to God.* For Protestants as for Roman Catholics and Orthodox, we go to church to a sacrifice: the sacrifice of ourselves (see Romans 12:1, R.S.V.: "your spiritual worship"). Spiritual gifts and material gifts are offered and are acceptable but only as they are tokens of our self-giving.

## Are we running with you, Jesus?

TEXT: "*As for us, we have this large crowd of witnesses around us. Let us rid ourselves, then, of everything that gets in the way, and the sin which holds on to us so tightly, and let us run with determination the race that lies before us. Let us keep our eyes fixed on Jesus, on whom our faith depends from beginning to end. He did not give up because of the cross! On the contrary, because of the joy that was waiting for him, he thought nothing of the disgrace of dying on the cross, and is now seated at the right side of God's throne*" (*Hebrews 12:1, 2, T.E.V.*).

Malcolm Boyd's book of contemporaneous, unconventional prayers has made us familiar with the phrase, "Are you running with me, Jesus?" It is good to convert the question: "Am *I*—are *we*—running with *you*, Jesus?"

1) Jesus is always ahead of us. We can never engage in a "Back to Christ" movement; it must be forward to Christ, advance with Christ. In his commentary on "The Acts of the Apostles," J. W. Packer quotes a writer on Luke's Gospel as saying that the picture of Jesus in this gospel is "essentially a journeying figure." "In Acts the comparable picture is of essentially a journeying church." *

2) Are we "running with Jesus" as the first apostles did

* *Cambridge Bible Commentary* (Cambridge: The University Press, 1966), p. 226.

in healing the sick and in restoring the spiritually dead (Acts 9:40; 20:9–12)?

3) Are we with Christ in being his agents of spiritual transformation? Are we transmitters of the Holy Spirit's power (Acts 10:45, 46; 19:5, 6)?

4) Are we running with the Lord Jesus Christ in mission to all the world, beginning in our own community, moving into inner city and suburbia, other regions of our continent, and then "into all the world"? "The journeying of the early Church in Acts was not only geographical. It also made its way among men of different races" (Luke 7:1–10 and Acts 10:1–8; 10:44, 45; 11:18).

5) Are we running with Christ in our interior life, in the life of prayer (Acts 1:14; 6:6; 16:25)?

## Strange gifts for God's children

TEXT: *"Endure what you suffer as being a father's punishment; because your suffering shows that God is treating you as his sons"* (*Hebrews 12:7, T.E.V.*).

Lent reminds us that the Christian's life is not all roses and that, as old Samuel Rutherford said two centuries ago, "If you have not got a cross, you have not got Christ, for the cross is one of the first of his gifts." Why is it so? Wiser persons are needed to satisfactorily answer. God our Father, says the writer of Hebrews, loves us and treats us as sons. This involves discipline and taking our share of hardship as good soldiers of Christ. Three simple metaphors are used in the New Testament for his strange gifts: (1) the burden—Galatians 6:5. And with the burden he gives resources. (2) The cross: Matthew 16:24. (3) The thorn. Galatians 4:13–15; 2 Corinthians 12:7.

## Gossip: harmful and helpful

TEXT: *"Words of thanksgiving and cursing pour out of the same mouth. My brothers! This should not happen!"* (*James 3:10, T.E.V.*).

1) What's wrong with gossip? Doesn't everyone gossip? Of course, some gossip is harmless. It can be a safety valve,

a means of relief. Dr. Leslie D. Weatherhead related the story of the Danish Arctic explorer Ejnar Mikkelsen who with his men spent two and a half years in the icy wastes of the north. They had no radio communication with the outside world. When he and his colleagues returned, he reported that worse than the intense cold and shortage of provisions was the dreadful silence of the desolate territory. "Our only relief," he said, "was gossip." *

But malicious gossip is far from an innocent indoor or outdoor sport or harmless relief. The Apostle James "laid it on the line," that it can be fed by the fires of hell. Gossip can be despicable, cruel, and murderous. Vicious gossip, slanderous remarks about another person, can murder that person's reputation and peace of mind. Read James 3:6–8. Jesus himself warned that on the day of judgment each of us will be held responsible for every careless word we utter (Matthew 12:36–37). Why do we engage in gossip? Is it because we are jealous, envious, consumed by selfish ambition (see verse 14 of this same chapter)? Is it because human nature perversely thinks that by pushing another down we hoist ourselves up?

What can Christians do? Resolve never to listen to rumors or transmit them when they reflect in any way on the character of another or of a movement or group. We must do more: we must let Christ live in our minds and personalities so that Christlike love can bar harmful gossip from our lives. ". . . love does not keep a record of wrongs; love is not happy with evil, but is happy with the truth" (1 Corinthians 13:5, 6). Long before Rotary Clubs framed and used their admirable test of "the things we think, say, or do," the great Alexander Whyte of Edinburgh said that all gossip should be subjected to three tests: (1) Is it true? (2) Is it necessary? (3) Is it kind? St. Augustine had inscribed on his dining room wall these words: "He who speaks an evil word of an absent man or woman is not welcome at this table." †

2) But gossip can be helpful. Think of the origin of the word "gossip." In Old English it was "god-sib." God was in it, and so was your kin, your "sib" (think of our word "sibling"). A gossip was one who sponsored a new Christian. You and I

* *The Eternal Voice* by Leslie D. Weatherhead (Nashville: Abingdon Press, 1940), pp. 167, 168.

† *Life of Alexander Whyte* by D. H. Barbour (London: Hodder and Stoughton, Ltd., 1921), p. 374.

can and must gossip our Christian faith. It is how the Communist party won many new members in China. According to John A. Mackay, president emeritus of Princeton Theological Seminary, party leaders had loyal Communists gossip about the communist ideology and program in the marketplaces of Chinese towns and cities. Something like this happened in the early years of the Christian Church. One Christian told another. Cannot we spread the news that our church is worth attending, our fellowship strengthening, our Christian concern and service worth sharing? "As the Father has sent me," said Christ, "so I send you." He sends us to gossip the Good News.

## Lord, are we peculiar?

TEXT: *"But you are . . . God's own people . . ." (1 Peter 2:9, T.E.V.).*

Are we a peculiar people? In the everyday meaning of the word "peculiar" the answer must be Yes. To many persons outside looking in, church members are really peculiar. We are still considered inhibited, too busy minding other people's business, "odd balls," "characters"—you can add to the list. They think of us as one woman said of another whom she disliked, "She is a good woman in the worst sense of the word."

Lord, we should be a peculiar people! That should be our prayer. However, we need to define that peculiar word "peculiar." In the King James Version, as in the speech of those far-off Englishmen who gave us the translation, "peculiar" meant "God's own people"; literally, "a people for God's possession." As such, we belong to God and therefore are highly privileged. As privileged, we have responsibilities. God's new people are to carry out the program left unfinished by his former people, ancient Israel. God loves us, and he loves us because we are a people owned by and dedicated to him, a community, not a heterogeneous collection of individualists. Once we begin acting as God's own people, some are bound to brand us peculiar. But as we live the Christian life of love and justice, of compassion and caring, they will wish for a great increase of such peculiar folk!

A British brother in Christ's service, the Reverend Arthur E. Dalton, found this verse of First Peter lending itself to a kind of memorable outline. His alliteration is not forced. We might think of his five "heads": (1) divided from the world; (2) dedicated to the Word; (3) divinely ordained; (4) different from the world; (5) delivered from the world.*

## Our God has wounds

TEXT: "*Christ himself carried our sins on his body to the cross, so that we might die to sin and live for righteousness. By his wounds you have been healed*" (*1 Peter 2:24*, T.E.V.).

A distinguished British Christian, the late Dr. Edward Shillito, wrote a poem during World War I which has spoken to more than one reader. It is entitled "Jesus of the Scars." In it are these four lines from verse four:

*The other gods were strong; but*
*Thou wast weak;*
*They rode, but Thou didst stagger*
*to a Throne.*
*But to our wounds only God's*
*wounds can speak,*
*And not a god has wounds but*
*Thou alone.*†

1) The scandal of the Cross is this, that on it suffered and died One who Christians claim was a unique disclosure of the living God. Dr. E. Stanley Jones once observed that the man-made image of God was one that typified strength and victory. Yet, when we meditate on the sufferings of Christ recorded in chapter 19 of John's Gospel, weakness and defeat befall the God who in the form of Jesus came down to this world. The passion of Jesus clearly demonstrated how God's strength was made perfect in weakness.

2) This "strong Son of God, immortal love" speaks to our condition because his wounds answer our wounds. He has known everything that you and I know about frustration, defeat, inner hurt, bodily weakness, rejection. And infinitely more.

* *Brief and to the Point*, p. 248.

† From "Jesus of the Scars" by Edward Shillito in *Masterpieces of Religious Verse*, edited by James Dalton Morrison (New York: Harper & Row, Publishers, 1948), p. 235.

"All the tides of the world's anguish were forced through the channels of a single heart." A literary figure writing to a friend about the terrific sense of loss his wife's death created said, "I will not be comforted by anyone who has not felt the like." Somehow we know that our Lord has "felt the like."

3) "By his wounds you have been healed." This is the glorious Good News of Christ's sufferings and death. Somehow he provides the "balm of Gilead" "which makes the sin-sick whole."

## Does God care?

TEXT: "*Throw all your worries on him, for he cares for you*" (*1 Peter 5:7, T.E.V.*).

1) *The atheistic facts of human experience.* A cartoon showed an irate father talking to his college-age daughter. He asks: "What kind of an 'in' crowd do you travel with, the in debt, the in doubt, or the in trouble?" Most of us travel sooner or later with the "in trouble" crowd. This is part of the price of being human. When the trouble cannot be shrugged off or laughed off, does God care? Does God genuinely care about families living in ugly squalor in slums? Does he care when an eagerly awaited baby is born with mental or bodily defects? When someone is struck down by accident or by some malignant disease? Does God care when men, women, and children are burned, wounded, killed in Vietnam or any other war zone?

When suffering is acute, or prolonged, what can the Christian say and do? Pious platitudes are an offense. If we talk about the nobility of suffering, we had better talk about it some distance from the bed of a sufferer. It is not physical pain that is the problem so much, thanks to anesthetics and sedatives, but it is the mental, emotional, spiritual pain. How can we reconcile this with a good, loving heavenly Father such as Jesus taught us to acknowledge and trust, and such as he trusted? It helps to delimit the area of the problem: suffering is a very private matter.*

2) *The affirmation of the Christian.* Does God care?

* See *A Religion for Agnostics,* by Nathaniel Micklem (London: SCM Press, 1966), pp. 128–42.

To this persistent question the Christian answer is, "Yes, God does care, and cares enough to identify himself with his child in his suffering and weakness. God cares enough to do something about it." So the writer of 1 Peter declares: "Throw all your worries on him"—on the God we know in Jesus Christ—"for he cares for you."

Indeed, perceptive Christian thinkers agree that the words, "he cares for you" constitute the central message Christ was manifested to reveal. This is the gospel: God cares for us. Because God cares for you and for me and for all his children, whether we believe in him or not, whether we are good or bad, we must care for others. The same God who was in Christ reconciling the world to himself is in Christ healing our hurts and wounds and sickness. Of course we have no adequate explanation of the problem of pain. There are insights such as George A. Buttrick sets down eloquently in his book, *God, Pain and Evil.** There are no completely satisfying explanations.

We may protest, as did Edna St. Vincent Millay, "I am not resigned to the shutting away of loving hearts in the hard ground!" † But frantic protest gets us nowhere. We must make our way through and beyond the pain and loss. We must take suffering seriously. We would not deny the grief, the agony, the defeat. We would turn over the burden of our anxieties and fears to the One who made us and redeemed us and loves us. He loves the burden. But how to do it? Where to go for certainty?

3) *The ascent to the event where assurance is given.* When we doubt that God cares, we must take our way to the cross of Jesus Christ. The cross stands as a sign not only of man's sin but of God's unending love. ". . . it was while we were still sinners that Christ died for us" (Romans 5:8). This is the proof of God's love. The cross is God's offering of himself to us; not just for us but to us. We need not an explanation of suffering but a victory. As James S. Stewart‡ said, the cross tells us that God is in it with us. Because this is true, we are in it with God. We can share in his redemptive activity and in his victory.

* (Nashville: Abingdon Press, 1966).
† See *Poems* by Edna St. Vincent Millay (London: Martin Secker & Warburg, 1956).
‡ See *This is the Kingdom* (New York: Charles Scribner's Sons, 1957).

## "The good God, he is so slow!"

TEXT: *"But do not forget this one thing, my dear friends! There is no difference in the Lord's sight between one day and a thousand years; to him the two are the same. The Lord is not slow to do what he has promised, as some think. Instead, he is patient with you, because he does not want anyone to be destroyed, but wants all to turn away from their sins."* (*2 Peter 3:8, 9, T.E.V.*).

The title of this essay was originally said with a sigh of resignation in which a trace of impatience could be detected. An older French-Canadian woman tending an invalid husband for many years was commenting on his physical vitality despite the loss of mental faculties: "The good God, he is so slow!" In the time when this much neglected New Testament letter was written, Christians who believed Christ's actual return was imminent were ridiculed for their naïve belief. The letter's author reminded his fellow Christians that the pagans "will make fun" of them and say: "He promised to come, didn't he? Where is he? Our fathers have already died but everything is still the same as it was since the creation of the world!" (verse 4).

So the apostle is reminding his readers that it is God's mercy that he does delay winding up human history. Professor William Barclay in his commentary on this passage writes that in this passage we may find "three great truths on which to nourish the mind and rest the heart." (1) Time to God is different than time to us (recall Psalm 90:4). God has eternity in which to work. (2) Time is always to be considered an opportunity to turn to God, to grow as Christians, to help our fellow souls. (3) God desires to give life eternal and abundant to all his human children (see Romans 11:32, 1 Timothy 2:4, Ezekiel 18:23).

## How to deal with our sin

TEXT: (*1 John 1:9; 1 John 4:10; James 5:16, T.E.V.*).

What to do with our sins? Explain them away as we will, they haunt us and become what current colloquialism calls our "hang-up." Not all guilt is morbid or illusory; we know that we have sinned. "A man knows, ma'am," said crusty old Samuel Johnson when asked why we should hold the idea that we are sinners, "and that's an end to it." In the New Testament are three statements among many others that give us guidelines for dealing effectively and therefore radically (at the roots) with this obstacle to wholeness and peace in living.

1) In John's first letter (1:9) there is the declaration attested as true by untold numbers of human beings. "But if we confess our sins to God, we can trust him, for he does what is right—he will forgive us our sins and make us clean from all our wrongdoing" (all that is evil, every kind of wrong). We will need more than a general confession of sin. We will not be completely honest unless we become specific. Is confession sufficient? Is there no place for restitution? Yes, whenever this is possible. But we cannot earn our pardon, our healing, or our acceptance. Moreover, sometimes confessing to God seems less satisfying than we had hoped. God uses human agents and instruments. Even if we are such stout Protestants that we repudiate every form of what is technically called auricular confession, we know how sharing our burdens with another helps us.

2) So the apostle of common sense who gave us the Epistle of James directs us: "Therefore, confess your sins to one another, and pray for one another, so that you will be healed" (James 5:16). True, discretion must be used in choosing the ones to whom we "tell all" as it was and remains. Having found a wise Christian friend in a pastor or physician, in someone who is shockproof and truly Christian, there is no therapy to equal this confession. Of itself this kind of confession must be completed by confession to the God of grace and love we know in Jesus Christ. What happens then? Then, as one translation of 1 John 4:10 puts it, our sins are canceled, blotted out, ended. ". . . he loved us and sent his Son to be the means by which our sins are forgiven." God sent his Son to be the *cancellation* of our sins. The old word is "propitiation" which has led many to suppose that Jesus offered his perfect life to appease an angry God. But it is God himself who makes possible the propitiation, and this, as P. V. Simpson makes clear in *Believing is Seeing,** is not something done *to* God, but something done *by* God to our sins. The meaning of Jesus' death is

* (London: Society for the Propagation of Christian Knowledge, 1958), p. 72.

not that it caused God to act differently toward his human children, but that it is God acting as he has always done, in such a way that it causes us to act differently toward God. ". . . God was in Christ reconciling the world to himself" (2 Corinthians 5:19, R.S.V.); or as in the T.E.V., ". . . God was making friends of all men through Christ." "The Cross brings into focus the meaning of Christ's life, sums it all up: it is the action in history of that which is taking place 'all the time' . . . in eternity. The cross is in God's heart." *

Through the cross we know God's love and we know that God's love cannot be defeated. The way of the cross is the way of resurrection. How deal with our sins? Acknowledge them, spell them out to a Christian counselor; confess them all to God, and appropriate his forgiveness and love. Then the unseen Lord will say in our souls what he said in his earthly life to the woman condemned for her sins: "Your sins are forgiven. Go, and sin no more. Go in peace."

## Hell is other people

TEXT: "*We know that we have left death and come over into life; we know it because we love our brothers. Whoever does not love is still in death*" (*1 John 3:14, T.E.V.*).

*But Judah said to him, "The man solemnly warned us, saying, 'You shall not see my face, unless your brother is with you'*" (*Genesis 43:3*).

1) "Hell is other people." This is the now familiar saying from the French existentialist Sartre's play *No Exit.*† An honest atheist, Sartre employs eschatology for the setting of his drama. Three lost souls occupy a room which they realize will be their lodging for eternity. Mutual confession of their guilt-ridden past induces mutual loathing. Yet, when escape is offered they refuse freedom. Each needs the other even when each hates the other. Sartre depicts these characters as having no eyelids. When we hate and mistrust other people we must live in sleepless vigilance lest our defenses be breached. Canon Theodore O. Wedel once asked if Satre's grim play is not a picture of the religionless world of our time. Beneath the thin

* *Ibid.*, p. 73.
† (New York; Alfred A. Knopf, Inc., 1947).

surface of human brotherhood without God and Christ there seethes a hell of anxiety, loneliness, suspicion, hatred.

2) True reading of our human situation confirms the biblical insight that *heaven* here and hereafter is other people as we see them through the eyes of Christ. No man is an island; we need people to realize and complete ourselves. Gregariousness and togetherness of themselves are not enough. We need people in the community of the Spirit—"in Christ." "He who does not love remains in death." Read 1 John 3:11–24; 4:7–21. A modern version of the parable of the Good Samaritan would have the priest and Levite saying to the beaten-up traveler, "Man, you need help, but I don't need you." But each passerby did need the wounded victim.

3) "We know that we have passed out of death into life . . . because we love our brothers" (1 John 3:14). Life at its greatest is life "in Christ," with God. To us God says what Joseph said to his brothers when they forgot the youngest boy: "You shall not see my face, unless your brother is with you." What about my brother of a different color, cultural background, economic bracket, political or religious ideology? How can he be "with me" and I with him? "Hell is other people?" Only when we reject, exclude, despise, or despair of them.

## How do you think of your church?

TEXT: *"From the Elder—To the dear Lady and to her children, whom I truly love. I am not the only one, but all who know the truth love you, because the truth remains in us and will be with us forever"* (2 *John* 1, 2, T.E.V.).

How do we think of the church to which we belong? Sometimes a church with a popular or prominent pastor is described as "Dr. So-and-so's Church." Occasionally it is designated as "my church." Disparagingly critics may refer to a living, witnessing congregation as "that church!" Here in this little New Testament letter, the Elder (imagine an ecclesiastic failing to give his own name or title!) speaks graciously of a particular church as "the dear Lady and . . . her children." Obviously the writer of this thirteen-verse communiqué has personified a particular church. Scholars are convinced that the writer is not addressing a certain individual. "The dear Lady . . . and her children" is the holy, catholic, and universal Christian church, the "bride of Christ" (Matthew 25:6 and Revelation 19:7). As such the church is the object of the heavenly Bridegroom's love (Ephesians 5:25). Although it is a "great mystery," Christ is also one with his church. John Calvin said that as Christians have God for their father, so they have the church for their mother.

Enlightening and inspiring would be a discussion of the four metaphors used in the New Testament to describe the character and work of God's covenant people. (1) The Household of God (Mark 3:35; 1 Timothy 3:15; Romans 8:15, 16; Romans 12:10; Galatians 6:10). (2) The Temple of God (Ephesians 2:20–22; 1 Peter 2:5). (3) The Body of Christ (Colossians 1:18; 1 Corinthians 12:12–26). (4) The Bride of Christ (Matthew 25:6; Revelation 19:7; Ephesians 5:25).

## Healthy-minded religion

TEXT: "*My dear friend, I pray that everything may go well with you, and that you may be in good health—as I know you are well in spirit*" (*3 John 2*, T.E.V.).

John who wrote the three letters bearing his name was a man of pastoral heart. However stern his messages might be, he never scolded his correspondents. Even his rebukes were written in love. In the opening verse of this letter John shows the concern of a true pastor for his friend Gaius. The apostle is sincerely interested in the physical and spiritual health of Gaius. Like his Lord and Master, John remembered that men and women have bodies as well as souls. Physical health is as much the Christian's concern as his spiritual and emotional health is. Today we realize that what God has joined together, soul and body, we must never try to treat separately. British minister and author Ian Macpherson gives three reasons why Christianity is healthy-minded. (1) Christianity is rooted in what Professor Donald M. Baillie called "the objectivities of our faith." Essential Christian beliefs are not subjective primarily, nor "dreamed up" by mystics. These express realities from beyond our minds and spirits. (2) Christ's religion is healthy-minded because it is socially minded. "The gospel turns *others* into *brothers*." Archbishop Coggan of York,

England, summed it up in an epigram: "The Christian faith views man not as a soul but as a whole." (3) Christ's religion is healthy-minded because it organizes itself into a community. The Christian life is personal but never individualistic. The church is integral to discipleship. "We are the body of Christ," and the community of the Holy Spirit.* A fourth reason is suggested: (4) Christianity is healthy-minded because it teaches the necessity of regular prayer.

## Steady as you grow

TEXT: *"To him who is able to keep you from falling, and present you faultless and joyful before his glory—to the only God our Savior, through Jesus Christ our Lord, be glory, majesty, might, and authority, from all ages past, and now, and for ever and ever!"* (*Jude 24, 25, T.E.V.*).

A signal from the ship's bridge to the steersman or engine room well known to sailors is "steady as you go." This directive assures the crew member involved that the ship's direction, speed, and general performance is to be maintained. Some of our enterprising banking institutions have adapted this signal for an advertising slogan: "Steady as we *grow*." The author of our shortest New Testament letter closes it with the ascription above. He commits and commends us to the everlasting God who is able not only to rescue and deliver his children from evil and peril but is able to protect us from these enemies of our spiritual and moral health and wholeness. Only as we are kept from falling into sin, into weakness of any kind, shall we be able to ". . . continue to grow in the grace and knowledge of our Lord and Savior Jesus Christ" (2 Peter 3:18). This is the key to true security and vital growth: to commit ourselves daily, sometimes hourly, and sometimes moment by moment to the divine Love and Power that will not let us go. The late Alexander Whyte of "Free St. George's Church," Edinburgh, once asked a mature Christian layman, "How are you keeping, Donald?" "Aye, Doctor," said the man, "I am no' keeping, I am kept."

The God we know in Jesus Christ is "able to keep you

* *Bible Sermon Outlines* edited by Ian Macpherson (Nashville: Abingdon Press, 1966), pp. 179-180.

from falling." More, he will keep you to the end and beyond and by his redemptive grace at last "present you faultless and joyful before his glory." A kind of "hallelujah chorus" breaks out in the soul of any Christian who realizes the source and presence and power of what has been called preventive Christianity.

## What Christ can do for us

TEXT: *"He loves us and by his death he has freed us from our sins and made us a kingdom of priests to serve his God and Father. To Jesus Christ be the glory and power for ever and ever! Amen"* (*Revelation 1:5, 6, T.E.V.*).

Of course the real question is: What can we do for Christ? To approach the Christian faith and life in terms of its utility is to prostitute the gospel. God is not a private or public service center. Nevertheless, more than one person at the end of his rope needs to ask someone who knows what trust in Christ, commitment to him, following him can do. The prophet John who gave us the last, strange book in our Christian Bible has a wonderful ascription which tells what he found Christ did for him. Remember that John was writing in prison, in an island concentration camp.

1) God in Christ loves us. Is there anything greater than to know you are a loved creature? God loves you, says Christ, going to the uttermost limit of sacrificial love to prove it.

2) God in Christ loosed you from the intolerable burdens, your failures, your guilt. He did it through his own death. Although we may never find an adequate theory of how Christ's death effects this deliverance, this cleansing, this liberation, millions can testify that in some mysterious way, as in John Bunyan's story *The Pilgrim's Progress*, when we come in sight of the Man on the cross, the burden of our sins rolls away and we need see it no more. Because God loved us first, he forgives us. To be "loosed" is to be made free. With a great price Christ obtained for us the freedom we need.

3) He lifted us. Come to think of it, that lonely prison on Patmos Island could not have seemed much like a palace or a cathedral. But, says the radiant Christian, Jesus Christ "made us a kingdom of priests to serve his God and Father."

A Scottish saint named Samuel Rutherford was imprisoned in Aberdeen, Scotland, for his stubborn loyalty to Christ. From his prison he wrote many letters to friends and parishioners. He gave his address not as the prison or penitentiary but "From my King's palace, Aberdeen." Rutherford was living in a palace, the home of his true king—Jesus. God means us to rule over all that is unworthy in us, and help others to gain mastery over every evil too. We are to be priests, too: to represent our fellows before God, to pray for them.

## Man is dead!

TEXT: "*To the angel of the church in Sardis write: 'This is the message from the one who has the seven spirits of God and the seven stars. I know what you are doing; I know that you have the reputation of being alive, even though you are dead! So wake up, and strengthen what you still have, before it dies completely. For I find that what you have done is not yet perfect in the sight of my God . . .'*" (*Revelation* 3:1, 2, *T.E.V.*).

For many a year now we have been aware that in the view of certain theologians and others, the death of God has occurred. True, repeatedly in history many human beings have acted as if God's death had occurred. Today there are not a few who proceed as if—as Mark Twain said when his obituary had been published—"the news was greatly exaggerated." (Whoever has not yet read Anthony Towne's delightful satire on the death of God, will find it on the back cover of the February 1966 issue of *motive* magazine.)

In the words of Richard Gilbert, "Reading Paul, Baillie and Barth reassures me that the D.O.G. heresy will not unduly shake the heavens." Mr. Gilbert then composed an uncommonly clever dialogue which might be added to Marc Connelly's *The Green Pastures*. In it Gabriel informs the incredulous God: "I swear—uh—state unequivocally that some young theologians are saying that your Primordial Totality has metamorphosed into the epiphany of immanence." God: "What does that mean?" Gabriel: "I don't know, but we've got Augustine working on it." When God asks how many people are affected "by all of this," Gabriel says: "Well, would you believe . . . maybe as many as four Young Turks who never had a pastorate." God: "What's a Young Turk?" Gabriel: "He's a theologian paid by the church to teach the opposite of what the church believes." God: "You've got to be kidding." *

It will not be earth-shaking to announce that Man Is Dead. The possibility has occurred to a distinguished psychoanalyst and author, Dr. Erich Fromm. Addressing a large convention of social workers, psychiatrists and psychologists in San Francisco, he remarked, "Theologians and philosophers have been saying for a century that God is dead, but what we confront now is the possibility that man is dead, transformed into a thing, a producer, a consumer, an idolater of other things."

In the first century of the Christian era, the prophet John made the same pronouncement concerning the church in the city of Sardis (see the text). Church members in that ancient secular city were affluent, smug, lethargic. They were dead, morally and spiritually, and evidently emotionally and intellectually.

1) We are dead when we no longer respond vitally to the stimulus of problems, of critical situations, of human need. Continuing his San Francisco address, Dr. Fromm said, "A man sits in front of a bad television program and does not know that he is bored; he reads of Viet Cong casualties in the newspaper and does not recall the teachings of religion; he learns the dangers of nuclear holocaust and does not feel fear; he joins the rat race of commerce, where personal worth is measured in terms of market values, and is not aware of his anxiety." †

2) We are dead when we permit hardening of the sympathies. We live in what may be called—in a nonecclesiastical sense—"Ember Days." The fires of concern have sunk into chilled embers. Said a nineteenth-century American essayist to a friend: "For God's sake, do not forbid the years to teach you tenderness."

3) We are dead when we are indifferent to God's purpose and presence in Jesus Christ within our world.

4) We come alive in this generation when we wake up. As Professor Anthony Athos of the U.S.C. says of the teacher: "This may be the age of the big cool, but the good teacher must burn hot."

* *Op. cit., Presbyterian Life.*

† *New York Times,* April 14, 1966.

In Revelation 3:1–6, the preacher will get further clues as to how Christ gives life to the dead now: Remember the teaching, repent, complete the work God has assigned.

## Enter God—when we open the door

TEXT: "*Listen! I stand at the door and knock; if anyone hears my voice and opens the door, I will come into his house and eat with him, and he will eat with me*" (*Revelation* 3:20, T.E.V.).

An early twentieth-century painting by William Holman Hunt became famous and familiar. It is "The Light of the World" and has been reproduced in many stained-glass church windows. Keble College, Oxford, England, has the original. Mr. Hunt was inspired by the words spoken by the exalted Christ in the book of Revelation. More than one has pointed out that the artist deliberately omitted a handle on the outside of the door. Christ does not coerce or compel. If the person inside does not open the door to the Lord of life, it may be that he does not hear, and he may not hear because he is not paying attention.

We, too, miss the touch of God upon our lives, churches, communities. If we are responsive and open the door, will God really enter? Christian experience answers Yes. It may be, as some scholars think, that the prophet John, who gave us this haunting verse, was writing the eschatological meaning, that the second coming of Christ was in his mind. We may also interpret this truth in personal, contemporaneous ways.

How does God in Christ enter when we open the door? (a) In humble, unconventional ways. He came first in strange simplicity. On one Palm Sunday, a British writer spoke of him as "a king on a ruddy donkey!" (b) He comes to eat with us. He comes in the sacrament of the Lord's Supper; he comes in meals in homes, in hospitals, in hostels where love is present. (c) He comes to disturb our peace and often to jolt our consciences (see J. B. Phillips' translation of Revelation 3:18–19). (d) He comes also as physician to heal. In Matthew's account of the first Palm Sunday, immediately following Jesus' visit to the temple, he adds: "The blind and the crippled came to him in the Temple and he healed them" (Matthew 21:14). He still comes to the temple to heal us of our self-despisings, of our guilt, of our inner hurts caused by failure, sorrow, rejection, disappointment.

## "Amen! Praise God!"

TEXT: *"The twenty-four elders and the four living creatures fell down and worshipped God who was seated at the throne, and said: 'Amen! Praise God!'"* (*Revelation 19:4*, T.E.V.).

In this vision of the prophet John, verses 1–10 of chapter 19 present the heavenly "spectacular" when heaven learns of the fall of Babylon, symbol of powerful evil. In these verses also are hints of preparations for the wedding of the Lamb and his bride. In the older, more familiar verses as well as in some recent ones there are the words, "Amen! Alleluia" rendered in T.E.V. as "Amen! Praise God!" Of course, "alleluia" or "hallelujah" means "praise the Lord," an expression of exultant praise often found in the Psalms and hymns and anthems. "Amen" in Hebrew is usually an affirmation concluding a Jewish or Christian prayer, meaning, "so may it be" or "so it is." Jesus used it in the sense of "truly" (see John 3:3). In Revelation Christ is called "the Amen" who is faithful and true. As James S. Stewart of Scotland and other preachers have pointed out, these two words may have meaning and incentive for us.

(1) "Amen" may mean "may God's will be done." Without attributing disaster, disease and sin to our heavenly Father, there come times when we must accept what comes to us and that which God can weave into the fabric of his design. "Amen" may also indicate a commitment to God's cause (see Luke 22:42).

(2) "Praise God!" These joyous words express the true faith in God (see Psalm 16:11). It also means assurance of God's victory (Revelation 11:15).

# Index of texts

*The 149 themes selected for exposition are based upon scripture texts from GOOD NEWS FOR MODERN MAN: The New Testament in* Today's English Version. *The order proceeds uniformly from Matthew through Revelation. The themes listed in the Contents (pages 3 through 6) are identified below by the complete scriptural reference and the corresponding page where it first appears.*